THE CYNICAL IDEALIST

DATE DUE

Highlight of an innovative peace campaign. John Lennon and Yoko Ono confer with Canadian Prime Minister Pierre Trudeau, December 23, 1969.

THE CYNICAL IDEALIST

A SPIRITUAL BIOGRAPHY OF JOHN LENNON

GARY TILLERY

QUEST BOOKS

Theosophical Publishing House
Wheaton, Illinois * Chennai, India

Quest Books
Theosophical Publishing House
P. O. Box 270
Wheaton, IL 60187-0270

www.questbooks.net

Cover photo © Bob Gruen / www.bobgruen.com
Cover design by Kirsten Hansen Pott

Every effort has been made to contact and acknowledge rights holders for all quotations
beyond fair use. We apologize for any unintentional errors or omissions and will correct
them in future editions of this book.

Photo: Pierre Elliott Trudeau, John Lennon, and Yoko Ono
© Library and Archives Canada. Reproduced with the permission of Library and
Archives Canada. **Source:** Library and Archives Canada/Credit: Duncan Cameron/
Duncan Cameron fonds/PA-175744

Library of Congress Cataloging-in-Publication Data

Tillery, Gary.
The cynical idealist: a spiritual biography of John Lennon / Gary Tillery.—1st Quest ed.
p.   cm.
Includes bibliographical references and index.
ISBN 978-0-8356-0875-6
1. Lennon, John, 1940–1980—Religion. 2. Lennon, John, 1940–1980—Philosophy.
3. Rock musicians—Biography. I. Title.
ML420.L38T55 2009
782.42166092—dc22   2009025756
[B]
Printed in the United States of America

6   5   4   3   *   10   11   12   13   14

Dedicated to

Aung San Suu Kyi
for her long struggle
to bring light

CONTENTS

AUTHOR'S NOTE

It would be foolish not to let John Lennon provide the soundtrack to a book about his creativity and thought. Certain songs stand out as key moments in the development of his philosophy and need to be discussed, but song lyrics lose their magic when freeze-dried and printed on a page. The written form will never be able to convey the nuances—for example, the pathos in Lennon's performances of "Mother" and "Cold Turkey," or the dark irony of hearing "Help!" delivered at an exuberant tempo. The key songs addressed in the text are listed at the end of each major section of this book and you are encouraged to listen to them.

ACKNOWLEDGMENTS

I would like to thank the authors whose research into John Lennon's life and work gave me a rich mine to work in the creation of this book. Deserving of special mention is Jon Wiener, whose long struggle to obtain government documents through the Freedom of Information Act (aided by the American Civil Liberties Union) should be applauded by all admirers of Lennon. While I didn't discover Wiener's *Come Together* and *Gimme Some Truth* until I was more than half-finished with this work of my own, I found his biographical material and retrieved documents particularly helpful in analyzing Lennon's views and activities during the years 1970–75.

I would also like to express my gratitude to the dearly missed Richard Lerner for his insightful comments on the first draft, to Seymour Shlaes and Will Marsh for their excellent editing, and to Sharron Dorr, Idarmis Rodriguez, and Nancy Grace at Quest Books for their diligent efforts to make this a better work.

INTRODUCTION

The catalyst that transformed this book from a daydream into a serious project was the reply to a question posed to a couple of college students. I happened to ask how John Lennon was perceived these days. Their response: of course he was well known as one of the Beatles, but—as with all pop superstars—he probably didn't deserve the level of fame he enjoyed.

Time may be clouding the image of John Lennon. If subsequent generations feel free to categorize him as just another celebrity, they need to be reminded of how extraordinary a person he was.

At the close of the 1960s, this pop superstar was recognized—in the company of world statesmen John F. Kennedy and Ho Chi Minh—as a "Man of the Decade." Lennon was the first rock star ever to hold an issue-oriented meeting with the leader of a nation. His opinion was so influential that an offhand comment during an interview in England sparked religious demonstrations across America. In fact, Lennon was such a highly regarded figure that when he moved to the United States from England Attorney General John Mitchell, Republican Senator Strom Thurmond, and the heads of the FBI, the CIA, and the Immigration and Naturalization Service all worked in concert to attempt to deport him in advance of the 1972 presidential campaign. Nor did his influence end with his death; some of the songs he wrote as a pop superstar are considered so politically charged that they *still* get removed from airplay at times of crisis.

However, this book is not a panegyric. John Lennon had his share of faults, as anyone who has read about him knows very well. For much of his life he overindulged in alcohol and drugs, tended to be abusive both verbally and physically, and existed in a self-centered fog that left him inconsiderate of the feelings of those around him. What he expressed as the "chip on my shoulder that's bigger than my feet" was mainly the result of a troubled youth, and to his credit Lennon frankly admitted his own defects in interviews (his passion for truth distinguishing him from almost all of his contemporary celebrities).

Although he was far from being a paragon, what deserves admiration is the tenacity with which he struggled to become one. He never gave up trying to transcend the type of person he had grown into and become something better. He kept reaching toward the ideal and along the way he left a string of creative achievements that resonate with others who struggle to improve.

This book focuses on those creative achievements, as well as on Lennon's comments and revelations in interviews. The purpose is to discover in them the underlying structure of his worldview and to present, in an orderly fashion, the insights he drew from life, the values he found important, and the principles he came to espouse. In short, it is an attempt to summarize the philosophy by which John Lennon lived.

The word *philosophy* is laden with the weight of twenty-five hundred years. We find it difficult to use without mentally conjuring the Wise Old Heads of history—from Plato to Kant to Sartre. We picture them musing about how to define reality and leaving us with exhaustively reasoned frameworks for understanding the "Truth." Unfortunately, we often feel that it takes an IQ of three hundred to understand those frameworks.

John Lennon's philosophy was that of a man of the working class who happened to see the world through the eyes of an artist, a man of restless intelligence who was willing to question *everything* about the foundations of his life and his society. He came up with his own insights, and, unlike the Wise Old Heads, he had a gift for communicating them in a direct way that we can grasp not only intellectually but also emotionally.

Lennon was attuned to his own time; thus his thinking encompasses postmodern isolation and anguish. The good news is that it also offers a way to reconnect. In the last years before he was murdered, he found a path out of the labyrinth of meaninglessness and rediscovered a measure of sunshine. He left a record of the process in his artistic creations and interviews. The aim here is to follow that process and examine the self-generated philosophy he managed to fashion out of a conflicted and turbulent life—a philosophy that elevates the human spirit and encourages us to take charge of our individual and collective destinies.

One early and revealing signpost of the process was a song he wrote in late 1965. Having enjoyed phenomenal success atop the entertainment world for two years, the Beatles released *Rubber Soul*, an album hailed as a creative breakthrough for the group. They had mastered the skills required to reach the top of the pop music charts at will and in their self-confidence felt comfortable striking off toward new horizons.

John Lennon contributed several memorable songs to the project. One was arguably the most self-revelatory of any song he wrote as a Beatle. He admitted in his 1980 *Playboy* interview that its message came straight from his subconscious: "I'd spent *five* hours that morning trying to write a song that was meaningful and good, and I finally gave up and lay down. Then 'Nowhere Man' came, words and music, the *whole* damn thing, as I lay down."[1] In stark lyrics about an unimpressive man confused about life, lacking any orientation and making meaningless plans, Lennon revealed inner turmoil that none of his fans could have imagined.

The twenty-five-year-old with fame and adulation enough for a lifetime, with worldwide respect for his creative genius, only days before a ceremony in which Queen Elizabeth II named him a Member of the Order of the British Empire and awarded him a medal coveted by the establishment, thought of himself as a "Nowhere Man" with no point of view, not knowing where he was going.[2] Lennon had fought his way to the top of society only to discover that the zenith was merely the nadir in a nicer neighborhood. He had eluded the "system" that molded young minds into useful parts of the socioeconomic machine, only to realize that rebellion against it had given him meaning while freedom from it left him directionless. He had escaped the angst created by an absent father and a sometime mother who finally vanished completely from his life, only to stumble into the cold embrace of nothingness.

Like the character in Edwin A. Robinson's poem "Richard Cory," Lennon was growing more alienated at the same time millions went to sleep envious of him. He confided to his close friend Pete Shotton: "The more

I have, the more I see, and the more experience I get, the more confused I become as to who I am, and what the hell life is all about."[3]

Fellow Beatle George Harrison had developed a fascination for Eastern religions, and at his suggestion Lennon tried to find answers in two of the sacred books of the East: the Bhagavad Gita, which crystallizes the essential beliefs of Hindus, and *The Tibetan Book of the Dead*, a Buddhist guidebook to the interim period between physical death and reincarnation. He also began a serious study of the Bible.[4] He had been an indifferent Christian when a boy, singing in the choir until he was finally banned from services for his irreverent humor and disruptive behavior. But now he needed something to believe in, a structure to make sense of his existence.

In reading the Gospel of Matthew, Lennon must have lingered over verses five and six of the sixth chapter, leading up to the Lord's Prayer: "And when thou prayest, thou shalt not be as the hypocrites are: for they love to pray standing in the synagogues and in the corners of the streets, that they may be seen of men. Verily I say unto you, They have their reward. But thou, when thou prayest, enter into thy closet, and when thou hast shut thy door, pray to thy Father which is in secret; and thy Father which seeth in secret shall reward thee openly." One night in the winter of 1966, unable to shake off the pall of meaninglessness that ironically had settled over him with his success, Lennon decided to follow the advice of Jesus. He locked himself in the bathroom at his home in Weybridge, outside London, then got down on his knees and begged for an acknowledgment, a sign, a revelation—from God, Jesus, or whatever form the deity might take—some hint that his appeal was being heard and some clue as to what he should be doing.[5]

But there was no response.

That unanswered appeal marked the beginning of a search lasting for a decade, an anguished search for an alternative foundation on which Lennon could orient his life. One of his defining attributes was a completely open mind, and his far-ranging existential quest generated the various images we now associate with him: dreamy-eyed proponent of love, flower-covered disciple of a guru, loudmouthed peace advocate, angry radical, despairing drunk, feminist. As a freethinker and iconoclast, he was bound to upset those who accepted the beliefs they had been handed while growing up. They found it hard to disagree with his goal of planetary peace and love, but they recoiled at his behavior, his contempt for accepted social norms, and his blunt opinions about religion, sex, marriage, nudity, racism, and other delicate subjects. Many dismissed him as a fool who had let unprecedented success go to his head.

John Lennon was no fool, although he didn't mind playing one if it called attention to his agenda. He was simply someone who saw the world through different eyes than most of his contemporaries—a genius. He struck out along his own path, paid the heavy price required, and left an influential body of creative work.

Throughout his search, and particularly after his union with Yoko Ono, Lennon never accepted the easy labels most of the public preferred to apply to him—a pop superstar or writer of popular music. His aim was much higher. While other songwriters of his era were satisfied with coming up with good, strong commercial songs, Lennon aimed at writing anthems. While others tailored their lyrics with an eye on mass appeal, he tried to express profound and personal insights drawn from the ongoing experiment of his life. His openly stated goal was to be measured against Shakespeare and Van Gogh and the other cultural giants who communicate across all borders, across all times—and he thought of himself as a philosopher.[6]

Can we consider John Lennon a philosopher?

If being a philosopher means systematizing one's thinking and conclusions into a unified whole, he doesn't qualify. But then, neither does Socrates. If Plato had not reconstructed his teacher's probing conversations with fellow Athenians into meaningfully arranged written dialogues, the philosophy of Socrates would have remained half-remembered bolts of lightning that had dazzled his supporters and infuriated his verbal sparring partners.

Like Socrates, Lennon did not leave behind a grand philosophical project of the sort produced by Aristotle, Kant, Hegel, Wittgenstein, or Sartre; he was a philosopher in the sense of being an independent thinker who did not hesitate to question what his culture expected him to believe, to arrive at other conclusions, and then to challenge his fellow citizens about *their* assumptions. Also like Socrates, he preferred to stimulate people to think for themselves rather than strive to teach them something they did not know.

From his own experience, he realized that our contemporary civilization puts little emphasis on independence of thought in the school years. The intent, by and large, is to educate new generations about the culture they live in and prepare them to be productive members of the system—not to create members of the working class who will enjoy breaking out of harness and challenging the status quo. According to Lennon, most adults continue on in their oblivion, "doped with religion and sex and TV," accepting the beliefs they have been handed and never attempting to find their own foundation. In the stark interpretation of Stephen Holden, they go about their lives "degraded and terrorized by institutions until they become self-deluded cogs, numbed by fear."[7] The only road to freedom most people appear to perceive arcs upward—that is, toward social and financial success, getting to the top.

Referring to himself, sardonically, as a "working class hero," Lennon shone a light on this process and asserted that he had found another path to liberation, even though he had suffered terribly for his refusal to conform. How much did he suffer, being a multimillionaire and one of the most famous and pampered men in the world? Bear in mind that at the time he recorded "Working Class Hero" Lennon had recently passed through excruciating heroin-addiction withdrawal and four months of Primal Scream therapy prompted by media ridicule and public condemnation for his unconventional lifestyle and quixotic efforts to bring world peace. In an echo of Jesus ("take up your cross and follow me") that most likely was conscious and deliberate, he ended the song by inviting listeners who were willing to pay the price of being a hero to do as he had done and follow him.

What did John Lennon discover along the path he encouraged his listeners to pursue? In his view, God is not some anthropomorphic deity with interest in our daily lives—one who smiles when we score touchdowns and scowls when we cheat on our spouses. He/she/it is a natural, neutral, universal energy that can be tapped for either good or evil purposes. Therefore, we are on our own, and daily life and world affairs should be human-centered.

Lennon thought that we ourselves have the power to reshape culture and world events if we will only recognize the fact and act individually and in concert. The first key to achieving this power is self-transformation. When considering how to improve the world, people almost always focus their attention outside themselves, which too often leads to resistance, confrontation, frustration, and defeat. Actually, the only thing over which we have control is our own attitudes and behavior. If we first focus on changing ourselves, internalizing love instead of possessiveness and violence, we take a small but significant step toward positive change.

Kindness tends to beget kindness; violence, violence. By being conscious of the impact of our attitudes and actions on those around us, we can begin, through a ripple effect, to influence the world, to "shine on." Further, by gathering together and functioning as a group of like-minded individuals, focusing our collective imagination on the society we want to achieve—the ideal Lennon referred to as the "absolute elsewhere"—he believed we could make it manifest.

For such fairy-tale thinking, it's easy to caricature Lennon as a wild-eyed idealist. That description fits—with one caveat. John Lennon was a *cynical* idealist. With the possible exception of a few politicians and billionaires, Lennon as a Beatle and ex-Beatle was exposed to more hypocrisy, duplicity, and hidden agendas than almost anyone on the planet. He was fully aware of the natural self-interest that hobbles our progress toward a better and more peaceful world. Despite that, he was optimistic that we could get there if we had a mutual dream and could keep it in focus—if we could, as a society, "imagine" it.

Setting aside the insights and conclusions Lennon himself reached, if we carefully examine his quest and his accomplishments we can still derive three useful guiding principles:

1. We owe it to ourselves to question the "truths" our culture passes on to us and to be cynical about the motives of experts and those in

authority. Each of us has the right to assess each situation based on our own accumulated knowledge and insights.

2. We owe it to ourselves to live our lives as though creating works of art, using the resources fate has dealt us. Happiness is to be found in spending the time fate allots to us at some endeavor we enjoy and participating in loving relationships.

3. We owe it to ourselves and to our posterity to aim at transforming ourselves, being aware of the ripple influence of our words and actions. We should contribute to the creation of the world we want to see, not some future we dread.

Much of John Lennon's creative energy was expended on efforts to wake us up—to open our eyes to new possibilities and our own potential. Though he never characterized it as such himself, he was arguably calling for a new Enlightenment.

The historical movement labeled "the Enlightenment" was inspired by a group of European intellectuals who believed that—because of the unchallenged beliefs instilled in them by parents, communities, nations, and churches—most people went through their lives in mental shackles. These intellectuals declared that it was time to move past doctrinaire thinking. Their goal was to raise human beings to the position of architect and judge of their own fate, employing the tools of science and reason.

In his own way, John Lennon echoed their call and shared their goal. An irrepressible freethinker, he managed to struggle free from the cocoon of his own culture and look back at it with objectivity. He achieved a self-generated viewpoint on his era and human life in general and he passionately wanted others to do the same. Excited by the possibility of global mental liberation, he took on the task, in his music and in his interviews, of being a catalyst in the transformation to a better world.

PART ONE

THE ROOTS OF
REBELLION

1

NOWHERE LAND

When John Lennon rose from his knees on that cold winter night in 1966, having followed the advice of Jesus and yet received no reply to his anguished appeal, he took the first steps on what would become a decade-long search for an alternative foundation for his life. His approach—independent, restless, and cynical—was in large part the product of his own personality.

His personality was in large part the product of his tormented youth. As a boy growing up in Liverpool, Lennon had found it difficult to maintain interest in academic subjects, but some lessons he learned all too well—among them being the precariousness of existence and the importance of self-reliance and self-definition.

The only remaining chance he had for a psychologically grounding adolescence vanished in one instant on July 15, 1958. That evening, when he was seventeen, his mother, Julia, had been having tea with her sister Mary Elizabeth ("Mimi"), at Mimi's home in Woolton, a suburb of Liverpool. After saying goodbye, she started toward the bus stop, two hundred yards away. She crossed the nearest lanes of Menlove Avenue to reach a median strip at the center of the road. A hedge ran along the median strip. Passing through the hedge to the opposite lanes, Julia stepped directly into the path of a car driven by an off-duty policeman.[1]

The death of his mother was the last, most traumatic, and most influential in a series of events that shaped Lennon's conflicted youthful psyche and would later drive him relentlessly to find his own truths as an adult.

He never really knew his father. Alfred ("Freddie") Lennon worked as a steward on passenger liners in the thirties, and after Britain entered World War II he served as a registered member of the Merchant Navy on ships transporting British troops and supplies. He was away at the time of John's birth on October 9, 1940, and the total time he spent at home in Liverpool between then and January 13, 1944, amounted to only three months.[2] In his absence Julia began to frequent pubs in the evening. The chance to sing, dance, and socialize was a welcome respite from sitting at home every night with young John. Seldom able to come home, Freddie finally accepted the situation and agreed that she should go out and have a good time while he was away at sea.

One day, when John had just learned to walk, Julia made her regular stop at the shipping office in Liverpool to collect the money held back for her from Freddie's wages. The clerk informed her that her husband had apparently jumped ship in America and disappeared.[3] She was financially on her own.

In reality, after a layover in New York City, Freddie had signed on to a ship he thought was bound homeward for England, only to learn subsequently that it would be headed for the Middle East. He missed the ship and was promptly interned by U.S. Immigration on Ellis Island, facing desertion charges. When he appealed to the British Consulate, he was offered the chance to avoid the charges by sailing on a ship headed for the Far East. He accepted, but then became enmeshed in further trouble when he was among several crewmembers arrested for stealing whiskey from the cargo. He served almost three months in an army prison in North Africa.[4]

Gradually, because of such absences, the bond of his marriage with Julia weakened. Until December of 1949, he continued to return home to Liverpool from time to time but was unable to reestablish his relationship. After being arrested in that month for an act of drunken vandalism that cost him six months behind bars, he learned that he could no longer qualify for work as a seaman and began to drift from one menial job to another.[5]

Julia, meanwhile, turned to other men. In 1944 she had an affair with a soldier, and a daughter by that union was given up for adoption in June

1945. A few months later she began seeing a hotel headwaiter named John Dykins, whom her family considered beneath her. Though she never divorced Freddie Lennon, she and Dykins set up house together.[6]

The couple could afford only a very tiny flat, and young John had to sleep in their bed at night. Julia's sister Mimi was scandalized by her behavior. As the eldest of five sisters, she felt duty bound to assure John a decent childhood. She visited Julia and suggested that she and her husband, George, be allowed to raise John in their home. When Julia rebuffed her, she appealed to the Liverpool Social Services Department. Investigators agreed with Mimi, deciding that the situation was unacceptable. In a home where the mother was legally married to a man other than the one acting as the boy's father, a boy of five should at least have his own bed, if not a separate room. Julia was notified that until she and John Dykins found a larger flat, John could not remain with them. She finally agreed and allowed Mimi to take John into her home.[7]

John was just getting accustomed to life with Mimi and George when, quite unexpectedly, Freddie Lennon made one of his reappearances. He telephoned Mimi one day and asked if he could speak with John. He invited his son to join him on a vacation at the seaside, up the coast in Blackpool. John knew his father only as some hazy, romantic figure who had gone away to sea and was naturally enthusiastic about the chance to spend time with him.

When the two did not return soon, Julia began a search. She turned up one day at the seafront boarding house where they were staying, explaining that she had tracked Freddie down through the help of one of his old shipmates. Instead of apologizing, Freddie stunned her with the announcement that he was preparing to take John along to start a new life in New Zealand. He invited her to come, too. Having no desire to leave John Dykins, she protested and insisted that their son would best be raised in Liverpool.[8]

John, just five years old, suffered through the test of wills by his parents. The father who had been missing from his world for so long now promised to take him for an adventurous life in a faraway land. The mother he loved and trusted pleaded with him to stay behind with her. Unable to decide themselves, they placed a terrible burden on him. Choose, they said, which future—which parent—he preferred.

The few days of having his long-absent father's attention had had its impact. John stated that he wanted to go away with Freddie. Julia pressed him to be sure of his choice, and he said he was. Only after she had tearfully kissed him goodbye and turned to leave did John change his mind and bolt after her.[9] He was not to see his father again until he was a grown man—and world famous.

Significantly, he did not keep his mother either.[10] Shortly afterward, Julia became pregnant by John Dykins. Instead of looking for a larger flat, the couple moved back into her father's home. Julia had a daughter in 1947 and another in 1949, and the temporary placement of John in Mimi's home gradually became permanent. From time to time, his mother came by bus to visit, but his aunt and uncle took on parental responsibilities.

Though he did keep in contact with his extended family, occasionally seeing and interacting with his half-sisters and cousins, and though Mimi and George Smith loved him and were diligent in rearing him, the virtual abandonment by both his father and his mother invited demons that hardened Lennon's personality. They were not exorcised until he was in his thirties—the torment they caused bleeding through in his 1970 song "Mother." And there was more to come.

Mimi, filling the role of mother out of a sense of duty, felt that it would be detrimental to his development to be too indulgent. Her husband, however, doted on the boy. She was the disciplinarian of the two, George the one who secretly commiserated with him and slipped him candy or a cookie. The owner of a local dairy farm, George Smith often took John on early morning visits to see his cows being milked. They enjoyed going on long walks together around Woolton. In the evenings it was he who most often put John to bed, reciting nursery rhymes to him, and John always insisted on giving him "squeakers"—kisses—before going to sleep. Over the years they developed a strong bond. Then one day, at age fourteen, John returned from a vacation to Scotland with another of his aunts to find that the ever-hearty George had abruptly vanished from his life, victim of a hemorrhaged liver.[11]

Only one thing helped assuage the pain of losing his Uncle George; not long before, John had begun to reestablish a closer relationship with his mother.[12] She and her new family had moved into a house only a short bus ride from Woolton, and John began to drop by to visit her—secretly at first.

Perhaps it was merely symptomatic of her character, or perhaps it was regret at being only sporadically involved in his life for much of his childhood, but Julia was very permissive with John, even when she knew he was dodging school to be with her. Also, unlike Mimi, she had an irreverent spirit and loved practical jokes. One of her favorites was to put on a pair of glasses that were missing the lenses and then enter into a conversation with the postman or a stranger. When the time seemed right, she would casually reach up and push one finger through an empty frame to rub her eye.

John began to spend more time with her, staying overnight and sometimes even "running away" to her home, spitefully telling Mimi that he was never coming back. When he became enchanted by music and acquired a guitar, he quickly drove his Aunt Mimi crazy with the sound but learned he was welcome in Julia's house. His mother loved music, played the banjo, and was constantly singing. She taught him the first chords he played on his new guitar, the chords she knew from the banjo.

The renewal of his close relationship with Julia had the potential to ameliorate the worst parts of his developing hard-shell juvenile personality—the caustic wit, the bitterness of spirit, the contempt for authority. With time, she might have guided him into a more positive direction by building on his impressive gifts—striking creativity, restless intelligence, a remarkable sense of humor, and a natural capacity for leadership.

She might have, but July 15, 1958, intervened.

After his mother's death, Lennon's response to the chronically shaken foundation of his youth was to thicken his defensive shell while going increasingly on the offensive. At first that consisted simply of directing his pain outward at those around him, teachers and schoolmates and even close friends, unleashing his sarcastic wit and picking fights with those he imagined had slighted him or felt sorry for him. In time, though, he came to channel the outbound energy into a drive to succeed in the one realm where he saw, however dimly, the possibility of eluding his own demons.

2

ROCK 'N' ROLL

The England in which John Lennon grew up was still staggering from the impact of World War II. The German Luftwaffe had repeatedly targeted the strategic port of Liverpool, leveling much of the city, and in fact John was born in the midst of a bombing raid.[1] He even carried a permanent reminder of the war in his middle name, Winston, which his mother bestowed on him to honor the indomitable British prime minister.

For a decade after the war, rationing and austerity remained a fact of life as the country underwent enormous convulsions. Industries organized for production of war materials struggled to retool for peacetime. The national debt tripled, and Britain became a debtor nation for the first time since the 1700s. The Labour Party, which defeated Winston Churchill and the Tories in July of 1945 and held power until 1951, undertook the radical transformation of Britain into a welfare state. The new government passed laws insuring benefits for maternity, unemployment, disability, old age, and death. It nationalized the coal, iron, and steel industries, gas, electricity, railroads, and the Bank of England. It also created the National Health Service, which socialized medical care.[2] (Lennon would one day make its standard-issue round-rimmed spectacles a fashion statement around the world.)

In the midst of these domestic transformations, the British Empire rapidly disintegrated. In one twenty-month span, India, the newly created Pakistan, Burma, Ceylon, and Ireland were granted independence, and the Palestinian mandate was relinquished, leading to the birth of Israel.[3]

The pillars of stability in this whirlwind of change were British values. The fortitude that had withstood Hitler's war machine had been vindicated. The traditions that had made Britain invincible had to be carried on. The guard at Buckingham Palace continued to change with clockwork precision. The new queen was crowned in 1953 with time-honored pageantry.

Educational institutions were expected to mold the new generation in the old ways. Teachers, even at such lowly institutions as Quarry Bank High School for Boys in Woolton, wore imposing black gowns, while their pupils were uniformed in a regulation scarf and a black blazer embroidered with the school emblem—a red and gold stag's head accompanied by the Latin motto *Ex hoc metallo virtutem* (From this rough metal we forge virtue).[4] Discipline was maintained through a time-tested system of detentions (an hour of chores after school), unpleasant visits to see the headmaster for worse offenses, and, as the last resort, character-building canings. This tradition-bound perspective awaited John Lennon when he came to Quarry Bank High School in September 1952.

He had spent his first six years of instruction at Dovedale Primary School, where for the most part he had been a diligent student, though even then he was displaying the characteristics he would be known for as an adult. The headmaster summed him up for Mimi: "He's as sharp as a needle. But he won't do anything he doesn't want to." A fellow student remembered: "If there was anything out of the ordinary going on in the school it was centred on him. You definitely noticed him, even at that age." Another commented, "You could register, even as a kid, that here was an oddball. Now I can see that he was a genius all along."[5]

At Quarry Bank High School, the academic system was divided into three streams—A, B, and C—with A reserved for those students who showed the most promise. Lennon did well enough on his final tests at Dovedale to qualify for the A stream, and he started off his secondary education in the company of the area's brightest youths. During his second year he was demoted to the B stream. By the end of his fourth year he was bumping along the bottom of the C stream. At the end of his fifth and final year, when he took the O-level examinations to determine his worthiness to go on to higher education, he failed to pass a single one of them. The headmaster of Quarry Bank wrote a dismissive note at the bottom of his final report card: "This boy is bound to fail." [6]

The problem was not with his initiative or intelligence. His Aunt Mimi owned a twenty-volume set of the world's best short stories, and by the time Lennon was ten he had read and reread most of them, being particularly enthralled by Balzac. At twelve he ploughed through her encyclopedia. By sixteen he had read the complete works of Winston Churchill. He also enjoyed Edgar Allan Poe, James Thurber, Edward Lear, and Richmal Crompton, and his favorite books were *Treasure Island*, *Alice in Wonderland*, and *Through the Looking Glass*. [7]

He had a precocious mind, and he was well aware of it. In a 1970 interview, he was asked:

Do you think you're a genius?
   Yes. If there's such a thing as one, I *am* one.
When did you first realize it?
   When I was about twelve. I used to think, I must be a genius, but nobody's noticed [*laugh*]. Either I'm a genius or I'm mad, which is it? "No," I said, "I can't be mad because nobody's put me away; therefore, I'm a genius."[8]

Lennon's academic problem was with academia itself. He felt stifled by the regimentation. He resented the assumptions that were inherent in the educational system—that those in charge had a right to direct his life, to tell him where to go and when to be there, to judge his work and his behavior by their own standards, and to expect him to study and master information *they* considered important.

So he rebelled against their authority. He played pranks to throw the system off balance. He would carry an alarm clock in his satchel, set to go off during the class, or rig the blackboard to come crashing down as soon as the teacher put chalk to it.[9] The class would erupt in laughter and be unmanageable for minutes, and Lennon would revel in the disorder.

The resulting detentions were considered a small price to pay for the satisfaction of rebellion, and they lost their effectiveness as a corrective when repeated several days a week.

Inevitably, he and his closest comrade, Peter Shotton, went too far one day and earned the dreaded caning by Headmaster Taylor. Even then, Lennon subverted the intent by capitalizing on an opportunity for humor. Between the headmaster's office and the hallway lay a vestibule. Passing through the vestibule on the way out to Shotton, who was still waiting for his turn, John dropped to his hands and knees and came crawling out the door, whimpering as though beaten into submission. Shotton was immediately petrified with fear, his imagination racing with what torture might be awaiting him inside. Then he noticed Lennon grinning at his reaction and erupted into an uncontrollable fit of giggling just as he was called in for his turn under the cane. Incensed at Shotton's lighthearted attitude about his punishment, Headmaster Taylor gave him the thrashing of his life.[10]

It was the first of many canings for the two boys, and eventually that method's lack of effectiveness drove the subsequent headmaster to inflict a punishment totally without precedent at Quarry Bank—ejection from school, which lasted for a week.

Lennon seemed congenitally incapable of conforming or reforming. The most obvious destination for a teenager with such a bitter heart and rebellious disposition was a sociopathic adulthood, and he might have ended there if he had not possessed a way to give vent to his frustration and yet maintain—at least in his mind and in the minds of those in his circle—a sense of parity. Lennon was not only extremely intelligent; he was also highly creative, and it provided him a way to cope.

While his instructors stood at the front of the room lecturing, he would sit at his desk scribbling, ostensibly taking notes. Actually, he was drawing caricatures of the teachers and writing poems and parodies of what was happening at school, creating works that were usually derogatory, often obscene, and frequently emphasized physical deformities. He would slip them to his classmates surreptitiously, evoking smothered laughter.

His output was so well received that he began to compile it in a special workbook he called *The Daily Howl*, which he added to each evening.[11] Each morning an eager audience would await the latest installment. The tome grew so popular that he was forced to draw up a waiting list of readers. According to Pete Shotton, the work had much the same flavor as *In His Own Write*, published in 1964. Reading the galleys for Lennon's first book of poetry, prose, and art, Shotton recognized some of the writing and cartoons from the days at Quarry Bank.

Lennon's poor grades at Quarry Bank made it pointless to try to enroll at any university, but another avenue was open. Everyone agreed that his drawings showed originality, and he applied to Liverpool College of Art and was accepted.

He started classes there in September 1957. He found a freer environment, with no dress code, and the agreeable requirement to make drawings of nude models. Yet the instructors were there to impart their own methods and expected their pupils to apply themselves to mastering them. Lennon, chafing under any constraints, soon resorted to his old tendency toward nonconformity. In one of his more memorable exploits, he worked diligently through a session as one of a class of fifteen students while the unclothed model held her pose. When the time came to hand in his effort to the teacher, Lennon's drawing depicted the one item she had been wearing—a wristwatch.[12]

The classmate with whom Lennon developed the closest relationship while in college was Stuart Sutcliffe, according to Mimi "the only real friend John ever had."[13] In some ways he was Lennon's antithesis—quiet, intense, diligent in his studies. But he was an uncommonly talented artist, and Lennon knew it; Sutcliffe was one of the few people whose opinion he took seriously. They became best friends and eventually roommates. When apart from each other, they would exchange letters that sometimes ran to twenty pages.

They had far-ranging discussions about art. Sutcliffe was obsessive about the subject, and he prodded Lennon to move beyond the cartoon-like drawings he usually produced and experiment with more serious works of oil on canvas. John responded by creating paintings described by another student as "wild and aggressive."[14] They tended to be set in darkly lit nightclubs and invariably included musicians and a blonde at the bar who resembled Lennon's dream woman, Brigitte Bardot.

Art held a fascination for Lennon, but the passion art inspired in Sutcliffe John felt for a radically different form of self-expression, one still in its infancy—rock 'n' roll. This new form of music appealed to his youthful vitality and his sexual energy, but most especially to his rebellious attitude toward tradition and authority. It had no respect whatsoever for tradition, and it strode right up to authority and punched it in the face.

Lennon first became conscious of the rock 'n' roll sound in 1956 while tuning in the faint signal of Radio Luxembourg, a pirate radio station broadcasting from the continent.[15] His initiation was "Rock Around the Clock," a record first released in 1954, then resurrected a year later as the title music for the film *Blackboard Jungle*. He loved the driving rhythm that was so far removed from the bland, syrupy music the BBC seemed to prefer.

He kept listening to Radio Luxembourg and one day heard "Heartbreak Hotel," performed by some boy with the exotic name of Elvis from the exotic territory of Tennessee. "Blue Suede Shoes" and "Hound Dog" followed, then a fusillade of pulse-lifting songs from other performers such as Little Richard, Chuck Berry, Eddie Cochran, and Buddy Holly. The music hit Lennon like a revelation, lifting his spirit at the same time it antagonized those in authority. The more the establishment disparaged Elvis Presley and the decadent form of music he championed, the more Lennon took them into his heart.

Britain had its own new music, skiffle, which energized American and British folk songs by applying to them faster tempos and harder rhythms. Skiffle's advantage lay in its simplicity and lack of polish. No need for lengthy musical training and a stage filled with expensive equipment; by learning three or four chords on a guitar or banjo and setting up a rudimentary rhythm on a hand-strummed washboard and a tea-chest bass, a group of aspiring musicians could start entertaining.

Lennon pestered Mimi until she took him to a music shop in central Liverpool and bought a steel-string guitar for seventeen pounds. In March

1957, he and a group of friends started a band. They practiced in Julia Lennon's bathroom or in an air-raid shelter in Pete Shotton's backyard—both favored for their acoustics. Their first public performance came on June 9, at the Empire Theatre in Liverpool.[16]

They initially called themselves the Blackjacks, but John quickly changed the name to the Quarrymen.[17] The reference to the school he was about to leave might have been sarcastic, or possibly even sentimental, but given his gift for wordplay it was just as likely a clever allusion to "digging rock." Soon after the group was formed, its repertory began to drift away from folk music toward rock 'n' roll. The driving force for this change was, of course, Lennon, who served as the group's lead singer and chief architect.

Still just sixteen, John Lennon was taking the first steps to find his own way—to decouple from the system whose aim was to channel him into a productive life. As of yet, he could not have understood it that way. His actions were merely intuitive rebelliousness—a combination of his own high intelligence, the self-assertiveness instilled by his unconventional family life, and his antagonistic feelings toward the traditions and discipline of the British educational system. Even so, though his group was simply an ad hoc assemblage of friends with washboards, tea chests, and banjos, he was striking off in a direction of his own choosing, the self-created leader of a group performing the type of music he most enjoyed.

He was groping to define *himself.*

On July 6, 1957, the Quarrymen played an engagement at the garden fete at St. Peter's Church, not far from Mimi's house. A friend of Lennon's, Ivan Vaughan, came to the event and invited a friend of his own named Paul McCartney. Between shows, Vaughan introduced them. Paul had brought along his guitar, and to establish his credibility he proceeded to play a song for John and his band. John marveled at Paul's musicianship— he was so impressed, in fact, that he overcame his fear of being outshone and later dispatched Pete Shotton to invite Paul to join the group.[18]

When the new school year began—Lennon at Liverpool College of Art and McCartney at the adjacent Liverpool Institute—the two began to meet during lunch breaks and after classes, practicing their instruments, working out the chords to the songs they liked, and attempting to write songs of their own. McCartney soon introduced Lennon to a schoolmate, George Harrison. In February 1958, he became a fixture in the band. The three of them met each day for lunch at the college canteen or in the classroom of Arthur Ballard, the one teacher who saw past Lennon's disruptive behavior and had an intuition of his potential.[19]

For two years the group struggled to keep together, to find local engagements, to pass auditions. Lennon kept up the pretense of being an art student, but his heart was in the band. He had little encouragement, other than the satisfaction of performing, but he continued to sense the possibility of avoiding the straitjacket toward which Mimi and the college and society were guiding him. To assure himself of independence, to avoid having to conform to the rules of others, to do something he loved instead of what was expected of him, he knew he had to succeed as a performer of the music the establishment despised.

3

HELP!

Lennon's friendship with Stuart Sutcliffe yielded unexpected benefits. Sutcliffe joined the Quarrymen at John's insistence, though he had no musical ability, using the proceeds from the sale of a painting to purchase a bass guitar. A friend of Sutcliffe's, Allan Williams, owned a small basement club, the Jacaranda. Williams allowed Sutcliffe's band to audition for the club and started to give them occasional bookings.[1]

The Quarrymen discussed changing the group's name to something more consistent with the leading popular bands, and Sutcliffe lofted the name Beetles—a nod to Buddy Holly's backing group, the Crickets.[2] Lennon, the wordsmith, decided that it should be spelled with an *a*, alluding to the driving beat of their music as well as to the Beat poets—Kerouac, Ginsberg, Ferlinghetti—whose charisma and antiestablishment attitude fascinated him.

In May 1960, Allan Williams booked the boys on their first tour, which gave the band its first glimmer of success. They traveled through Scotland as the backup group for a local singer. Later that same summer, Williams was also responsible for the booking that proved pivotal to their development—Hamburg, Germany.[3]

Situated in the city's red-light district, the Indra and Kaiserkeller clubs attracted a mélange of dockworkers, gangsters, middle-class men seeking a respite from their wives, and university-age boys and girls with bohemian inclinations. The atmosphere was raucous, combustible, often menacing. Confrontations were frequent, fights regular, and the waiters, who doubled as bouncers, all carried truncheons and pistols that ejected small clouds of tear gas.[4] Customer tables crowded the stages, and entertainers came within easy reach of heckling, drunken patrons. Those who survived were the ones who learned to show no fear, and those who succeeded learned to project boundless self-confidence—even to be confrontational with the audience.

Lennon flourished in the chaos. "I grew up in Hamburg, not Liverpool," he asserted.[5] Up to the time he left Liverpool College of Art in July 1960, his approach to life had been one of simple rejection—of the system itself, of the authorities responsible for making him conform to the system, and of the processed information he was expected to assimilate. In Hamburg, he suddenly found himself with nothing to reject and license to be free. Nothing was expected of him other than to perform the music he loved.

"To do is to be," Sartre asserted. In the dark, turbulent world of the Indra and the Kaiserkeller, Lennon began constructing his adult persona on the irreverent personality he had formed as an adolescent.

The owner of the clubs gave him free rein, knowing that the patrons drank more when entertained by a flamboyant show. Lennon refused to defer to them, responding to their rowdy taunts with a *Seig Heil!* and a Nazi salute.[6] He honed his sarcastic humor ("Where's your tank?"), which he shouted out in English amid the din so the listeners usually did not realize they were being skewered.[7] He played the fool himself, coming on stage in his underwear and sporting a toilet seat around his neck. He drank during numbers, smoked, ate, threw food, and stopped dead in the middle of a song when he lost interest.

He began defining himself as a creative entity, too, maturing as singer, performer, and songwriter. Playing from six to eight exhausting hours a night with his group, he learned how to catch the attention of a chaotic crowd, to create rhythms that could not be ignored, melodies that echoed in the brain.

Lennon also encountered the "street" version of existentialism. Its most famous proponent, Jean-Paul Sartre, had been lionized by continental intellectuals ever since World War II. University professors debated his philosophy and disseminated it through their students. While many students no doubt struggled to grasp its nuances, they were disillusioned with the political and economic ideologies that had come to dominate society and embraced the philosophy's underlying call to define themselves.

Among his college friends back in Liverpool, Lennon had spent many lively hours after classes discussing the Beat Generation and its motivations.[8] Now, when he struck up friendships with some of the younger visitors to the Kaiserkeller, he found that they, like him, felt alienated within their own culture. They were art students from Hamburg's Meister Schule, a group that deliberately turned its back on established values, generated its own rules for behavior, and held its own view of art, music, and fashion. Lennon quickly dubbed the group "the exis." Klaus Voormann first came in, alone, after a clash with his girlfriend, Astrid Kirchherr. He enjoyed the Beatles' performance so much that three days later he brought her to the club to see them. Within two months, Astrid and Stuart Sutcliffe had become engaged. Lennon became good friends with Astrid and her circle and often visited her home, gravitating to her bookcase and expressing such interest in certain volumes that she would purchase English-language editions for him.[9]

The Beatles' first visit to Hamburg lasted scarcely more than one hundred days, but it fundamentally altered Lennon. From his letters back home to his girlfriend, Cynthia Powell, she could clearly see that while his drive to succeed remained red hot, the frustration and anger she had witnessed in Liverpool was noticeably reduced.[10]

The experience came to a premature end when the owner of a more prestigious club, the Top Ten, offered the Beatles more money and better accommodations. They broke their contract with the owner of the Kaiserkeller, Bruno Koschmider, and he determined to get even. He notified the police that George Harrison, not yet eighteen years old, was working illegally in the country, and he was summarily deported back to Britain. Koschmider also charged McCartney and the group's drummer, Pete Best, with starting a fire in the lodgings he provided them, and they too were forced to leave after spending several hours in jail.[11] With the band broken apart and no money put away, Lennon reluctantly followed the others home to Liverpool in December 1960.

After a few morose weeks, he summoned up the spirit to renew the up-hill battle. Pete Best arranged for them to play at the Casbah, a basement club owned by his mother.[12] They also had several engagements at Litherland Town Hall, where the fans who remembered the group from before Hamburg were amazed at the transformation. But the real coup came in the spring of 1961, when the group managed to get booked into a dank cellar in the heart of the business district of Liverpool.

The place was called the Cavern. Secretaries and sales clerks liked to gather there at midday for a quick lunch and the chance to listen to live jazz music until it was time to get back to work. Now, to a startled crowd of white-collar workers hoping merely for a respite from their humdrum jobs, the Beatles suddenly brought the high-voltage energy of a late-night set of rock 'n' roll in Hamburg.[13]

The first Beatles performance at the Cavern took place on March 21, 1961. The last would come on August 3, 1963.[14] In that span of time, they would progress from being popular noontime entertainers in Liverpool to nationwide stars, reaching the pinnacle of the music charts with both a single and an LP.

In April 1961, they were offered the chance to return to Hamburg, this time to play in the Top Ten Club. One of the other performers there was Tony Sheridan, a solo singer for whom they often played backup. A German record producer happened to come into the club one night when they were playing together and liked what he heard. He wanted to record Sheridan, and Sheridan said he would be most comfortable in the studio if the Beatles backed him, so they were all signed. One of the songs recorded, "My Bonnie," charted in Germany and played a pivotal role in the Beatles' rise to fame.

When they returned to Liverpool (minus Sutcliffe, who stayed behind with Astrid), the Beatles brought back copies of "My Bonnie," which was just being released in Germany. Paul lent his to the disk jockey at the Cavern, Bob Wooler, who played it during breaks and at other venues. On Saturday, October 28, 1961, a customer who had heard Bob Wooler recommend the song the previous night at Hambleton Hall walked into a record shop near the Cavern and asked the manager, "Have you got a disk by the Beatles?"[15]

Brian Epstein had never heard of the record and had none in the store, but he made a note to try to order one on Monday. Before he could do so, two girls came into the store that same day and made the same request. Making inquiries, he was surprised to learn that the Beatles were giving lunchtime performances just a couple of hundred yards from his shop. He had actually seen them before, a scruffy troop of teenagers who came to his shop and browsed through his record racks.

Epstein finally visited the Cavern on November 9 and was stunned by the band's magnetism and the excitement they generated. He was particularly impressed with the leader of the group, John Lennon. On December 3, 1961, Epstein offered to manage the band.[16]

The year 1962 started with failed auditions and uniform apathy at the record labels Epstein approached. One piece of professional wisdom became legendary: "Not to mince words, Mr. Epstein, we don't like your boys' sound. Groups of four guitarists are on the way out."[17] About to give up hope, Epstein finally secured a penurious contract with Parlophone, a lowly division of the giant recording company EMI. The label's recording manager, George Martin, informed Epstein that while he thought the group had possibilities, he wanted to use a session drummer for the upcoming studio recordings.

John, Paul, and George saw the request as the opportunity to replace Pete Best. For reasons never made completely clear, but which seemed to stem from a difference of personality and envy over Best's good looks and popularity with the fans in Liverpool, they were content with his departure. In August, Epstein gave the news to Best, and to take his place Lennon invited a drummer well known to all three Beatles—Ringo Starr.

On September 4 they recorded their first single for their new label, a song McCartney had started as a teenager and Lennon had recently helped finish by working on the middle section.[18] "Love Me Do" was heavy on beat, simplistic in its use of instruments, and trite in its lyrics. The intent was simply to create for the marketplace. Though Lennon was the elder partner of the songwriting duo, he was still only twenty-one, and at this point his only goal was to exploit the opportunity he had been given to break into the business of rock 'n' roll. The words and ideas expressed in the lyrics were secondary. Above all, he wanted to validate the dream he had been pursuing to the detriment of his education and Aunt Mimi's expectations.

In late October, "Love Me Do" entered the British Top Thirty chart and eventually reached number seventeen.[19] Encouraged, George Martin called the boys back into the studio to record again.

They wanted to try "Please Please Me," a song Martin had previously rejected at the time of the "Love Me Do" sessions. Lennon had written it in emulation of Roy Orbison, and they demonstrated it for Martin in an Orbisonesque tempo.[20] Their new version, faster paced, ran through the whole song in just over a minute. Martin made suggestions that expanded it to a more appropriate length, and they breezed through the recording with the revised arrangement. Martin pressed the intercom button the moment they finished: "Gentlemen, you have just made your first Number One."[21]

By late February his prediction had proved accurate, and the success of the record marked the start of the most phenomenal rise to fame in music history. Within eighteen months, the Beatles had a string of hits at the top of charts on both sides of the Atlantic (at one point the five best-selling records in the United States were *all* by them), they had starred in a feature film that was both a commercial and a critical success, the word *Beatlemania* had entered the lexicon, John Lennon had written and published one of the top-selling books in the world, and the four of them had become among the best-known, most-discussed, and most-reported-on individuals alive.

During this period Lennon was obsessively focused on continuing the momentum. When his son Julian was born in April 1963, he was on tour and didn't visit the hospital for a week.[22] Following "Please Please Me," the Beatles had a string of number one hits. They wrote constantly to fill out albums and generated a number of popular classics. These uniformly relied on a strong beat and infectious melodies for appeal. Some songs included clever wordplay, but the lyrics remained of minor consequence. Their subject matter adhered to the basic themes of popular music and of adolescent concern—love and loss. It did not occur to Lennon to introduce serious ideas into his creations. To him songwriting was still a craft, not an art, and his only goal was to equal the commercial appeal of Buddy Holly and the Everly Brothers.

Beatles music triumphed in the United States, at least in terms of sales. But contemporaneous with their success a rival figure emerged in America who pushed the horizons of popular music back to distances unimaginable only a few years before. Into the shallow pop song milieu, he introduced mature, thought-provoking subjects and sophisticated, poetic lyrics.

Bob Dylan rose to fame through the medium of folk music, in which songs were often commentaries on social conditions and lyrics were often crafted to deliver a message. With a gift for both words and melody, Dylan had mastered the medium, creating works of intellectual and emotional potency—"Blowin' in the Wind" and "With God on Our Side," among many others. However, folk music was a medium he employed, not a category in which he placed himself. Like John Lennon, he had come of age at the dawn of rock 'n' roll, and he also appreciated the soulful appeal and gravel-road authenticity of blues music.

Drawing on these, and on his friendship with Allen Ginsberg and other poets—as well as on influences gleaned from his wide reading, especially the French Symbolists—Dylan was about to break away from the confining traces of folk music and create something new, something that fused all of these seemingly unrelated forms of art into popular music in which the listener realized he or she was being addressed not just as a consumer with a heart or a groin to stimulate, but as an intelligent being. Dylan's songs were filled with literary allusions, compelling metaphors, tantalizing ambiguities—and he expected listeners actually to *think* about what they were hearing.

Inevitably, as two dominant forces in the music scene, Dylan and the Beatles got together. The five were introduced in August 1964 at a New York hotel. Lennon had just published *In His Own Write* and was considered "the intellectual Beatle," and Dylan was especially interested in spending time with him. After some awkward conversation, Dylan suggested that they all slip away to smoke some marijuana.[23]

Lennon, never having experienced "grass" before, savored the mind-altering effect. The mellow feeling he got while smoking it neutralized the bitterness with which he coped with the world, paved the way for his experimentation with more potent drugs, and began a gradual process of personality change that prepared him to be a leader of the "peace and love" movement later in the decade.

However much he was willing to credit Dylan with opening his mind, Lennon downplayed Dylan's influence on his own music. When Dylan played his newly recorded songs for him and said, "Listen to this, John," and "Did you hear the words?" Lennon claimed he would respond, "That doesn't matter, just the *sound* is what counts. The overall thing."[24]

This assertion may have been partly true, since what enchanted Lennon about music was his physical reaction to what he heard. But perhaps Lennon, with his own facility for language, was awed by the level of poetry Dylan achieved and felt uncomfortable that his own lyrics of that time seemed so adolescent.

The summer of 1964 marked the beginning of a troubling period for Lennon. Ever since the formation of the Quarrymen in 1957, his obsession had been to succeed in a rock 'n' roll band, and his secret dream had been to make it to the top of the rock 'n' roll world. Brian Epstein, in his efforts to promote the Beatles, had made a prediction he truly believed, but which sounded like outrageous bluster—that one day the group would be "bigger than Elvis." Now, only seven years since the Quarrymen had first performed in public and less than three years after the record store manager had walked into the Cavern to see the Beatles play, Lennon's secret dream and Epstein's claim had come true. No one on the planet, Elvis Presley included, approached their fame and influence.

The group lived a charmed existence—in the center of a media hurricane, the target for a torrent of invitations and offers from every stratum of society, while income streamed in from recording and songwriting royalties, a hit movie, live concert performances, and a percentage on the sales of a myriad of Beatle-related products. At the age of twenty-three, Lennon had everything.

Unexpectedly, he found that everything was not enough.

Contemporaneous with his meeting with Bob Dylan were inklings of a new maturity in Lennon's songs and the first shadow of disenchantment. Curiously for a man envied by millions of fans around the world, he wrote a song called "I'm a Loser." He characterized himself as wearing a mask ("I'm not what I appear to be") and punctuated self-pitying lyrics with Dylanesque harmonica riffs.

The depiction of the Beatles' harried life in *A Hard Day's Night* was close to their reality in 1964. The concept for the film came from a Lennon quip to the director, Richard Lester, who asked how he liked the group's recent visit to Sweden. "Oh, it was a room and a car and a car and a room and a room and a car."[25] Throughout 1964 and 1965, that described their world—a claustrophobic existence played out at a frenetic pace.

They tried to savor their success, having reached the pinnacle after a tough climb and imagining that, like other pop stars before them, they would soon face a steep descent on the other side. But success turned out to be a monster with a voracious appetite. Rival bands were intent on knocking the Beatles off the summit. To maintain their preeminence, they had to come up with new songs, better songs, and doggedly promote them. When they were not in the studio or on concert tours, their days were filled with interviews, photo shoots, and personal appearances. Lennon found his life revolving around material considerations and the Beatles' standings in the charts.

When not on tour, he took refuge with his wife, Cynthia, and son, Julian, at Kenwood, his home in Weybridge, an affluent suburb of London. There he worked on his songs and the poetry, prose, and illustrations that would be published as his second book, *A Spaniard in the Works*. Another diversion was reading. Cynthia recalled him poring over Tennyson, Swift, Tolstoy, Oscar Wilde, and Aldous Huxley.[26]

He began increasingly to stay home when possible, unless it was to visit the home of one of the other Beatles, deterred partly by the prospect of being hounded by fans and partly by his natural indolence. He slept long hours, late into the afternoon, and owing to his self-indulgent lifestyle and a diet slanted toward the fatty foods of his Liverpool youth, he began to gain weight. (He would later refer to this as his "Fat Elvis period.")

Pete Shotton, who maintained contact with him and spent weekends and often whole weeks at his home, witnessed his steadily growing insularity, and, with it, introspection. During this period Lennon confided to him, "The more I have, the more I see, and the more experience I get, the more confused I become as to who I am, and what the hell life is all about." Seeking some direction, or at least a compass, Lennon began to study the works of Sigmund Freud, C. G. Jung, and Wilhelm Reich.[27]

In America, Bob Dylan was in the process of redirecting the flow of popular music. In early 1965 he released the revolutionary album *Bringing It All Back Home*. In its eleven tracks Dylan made the transition from folk to rock, creating classics such as "Subterranean Homesick Blues" and "Mr. Tambourine Man." He then topped that achievement in August with the album widely considered to be his greatest masterwork, *Highway 61 Revisited*, in which he performed a feat previously unimaginable—employing rock 'n' roll to create high art.

Lennon downplayed Dylan's influence on him in interviews at the time, but Pete Shotton recalled that when Lennon listened to records at his Weybridge home, he listened "above all" to Bob Dylan. According to Shotton, "Dylan's initial impact on John was almost comparable to that of Elvis Presley a decade earlier."[28] No one anywhere could match Dylan's lyrics—the improbable fusion of surreal imagery and streetwise idiom—but his audacity prodded Lennon and other contemporaries to aim higher in writing popular songs that were thought provoking and poetic.

Just a few weeks prior to the debut of *Highway 61 Revisited*, the Beatles released their album *Help!* It was a strictly commercial product, intended to support the film of the same name, and included their staple—breezy, up-tempo love songs. However, it included three curiosities.

The one that attracted the most attention was "Yesterday," a song whose doleful sentimentality was rendered innovative by the use of a string quartet. The tune astonished everyone by its popularity and ended up becoming the most covered of all Beatle songs. Lost in its shadow was

"You've Got to Hide Your Love Away," ostensibly just another love song but actually an acoustic confession in which Lennon acknowledged his difficulty in letting his true feelings show. The lyrics had a Dylanesque quality, and Lennon ultimately admitted in a *Playboy* interview shortly prior to his death, "That's me in my Dylan period."[29] Perhaps without even being aware of it, he was groping to find a way to reveal the process of his own self-examination through his music.

The third curiosity was a remarkable example of "hiding in plain sight"—a melancholy revelation embedded in the upbeat title song of the film and album. In simple lyrics, Lennon openly expressed the profound malaise he was feeling, the lack of a foundation and his growing Richard Cory–like despair in the midst of wealth and adulation.

No one realized it at the time, not even Lennon. He wrote "Help!" merely because no one cared for the working title of the Beatles' second film, *Eight Arms to Hold You*, and, just as they were completing filming, some exasperated crew member had suggested *Help!* as an alternative. When he brought the slow song into the studio, the band tried it in a stepped-up tempo and found that it made an excellent title track.

To Beatles fans the song was just another in a string of joyous, dance-friendly hits. Its revelations about inner turmoil, about feeling insecure and needing someone, and its open appeal for help ("Won't you please, please help me?") were lost, even on Lennon. Not until later in his life, looking back, did he realize that the title and the plaintive lyrics had been a cry from the heart.

Three months later "Nowhere Man" would pop up out of his subconscious mind, words and music together, a finished song, and soon after that he would be down on his knees in a locked bathroom begging God for a sign.

Suggested Listening
  "Nowhere Man"
  "Help!"
  "Mother"

PART TWO

THE LONG, DARK CYNICAL NIGHT

4

GOD

John Lennon's dark night of the soul, which ironically commenced with his incandescent success, would not fully lift from him for another decade. He struggled through what Viktor E. Frankl called the "existential vacuum," the state in which individuals "are haunted by the experience of their inner emptiness, a void within themselves."[1]

A psychiatrist who survived Auschwitz and devoted his career to addressing the problem of meaning, Frankl summed up the predicament of a modern person in his book *Man's Search for Meaning*: "No instinct tells him what he has to do, and no tradition tells him what he ought to do; sometimes he does not even know what he wishes to do." Frankl maintained that the individual can fill the void of meaninglessness only by discovering "for what, to what, or to whom he understands himself to be responsible."[2] The answer is different for every person, and discovering that answer becomes a challenge each person has to pursue in his or her own way.

Lennon had slipped into the existential vacuum as a result of exile from his parents. He plunged further by lashing out in his pain, summarily rejecting what most well-adjusted children take for granted—authority and tradition. He chose his own nonconformist path, striving to build a life around a form of music not approved of by the establishment.

As a result of his own inherent talent and genius, his choice of bandmates, good luck, and sheer single-mindedness, Lennon achieved incredible success. He survived in Liverpool, defined himself in Hamburg, and then subsequently conquered London and America to become one of the leading creative forces in popular culture.

He had surmounted gravity, rocketed through the confining atmosphere, and burst out into the freedom of open space. But now, with the ascent safely behind him, he could focus on other things, and he discovered the sterility of complete independence. Free to move in any direction, he was adrift, feeling responsible to no one but himself and so feeling alienated.

Lennon had been amply rewarded for his youthful rebelliousness with wealth, fame, and prestige; that he continued to employ the same approach as an adult was therefore not surprising. He possessed a drive to discover his *own* foundations, and that meant questioning everything his culture had handed him to believe and questioning the motivations of those who claimed to have answers. His sense of spiritual desperation made him receptive to guidance from any direction, but his ruthless self-honesty meant that he could not for long leave assumptions unchallenged, no matter how much solace he gained from a particular solution.

Not long after his unanswered appeal to God in the winter of 1966, Lennon read a book on Jesus that had a powerful effect on him. In fact, it would have immense consequences for all of the Beatles, leading to the most nerve-wracking tour they ever experienced and the end of their live performances together.

The previous year, a British scholar who had been part of the original team that studied the Dead Sea Scrolls, and who subsequently carried out his own translation of the New Testament, published a book offering laymen a myth-free view of the life and mission of Jesus. He gave it the incendiary title *The Passover Plot*.

A Jew himself, Hugh Schonfield interpreted Jesus within the context of the Jewish milieu of the first century. The book's thesis was that Jesus was an extraordinary man, brilliant in his knowledge of the Torah and in his ability to understand and outwit his adversaries, who held an obsessive belief that he was the instrument chosen by God to deliver his people from their oppressors and inaugurate the Kingdom of God on earth. In short, he was convinced that he was the Messiah as predicted by the scriptures.

He felt that in him many of the prophecies were fulfilled and that he had been given the intelligence and foresight—and the *duty*—to contrive to make the others come true as well.

Schonfield cited many examples, but one will suffice.[3] Just before his entry into Jerusalem—the final, triumphal entry in which he would be hailed by his ecstatic followers as the Messiah and begin the Passion Week—Jesus and his entourage, arriving from Galilee, approached an outlying hamlet called Bethphage. He directed two of his disciples to proceed there ahead of the group and look for a tethered colt of an ass, one that had never been ridden. When they encountered this colt, they were instructed to untie him and bring him back, and if anyone challenged what they were doing, they were simply to say, "The master needs him."

Obediently, they carried out the wishes of Jesus. The colt was there precisely as he had foreseen, and they brought it back, no doubt in awe of his display of clairvoyance. As he mounted the colt to ride into Jerusalem, the more perceptive of his followers realized that through that act he was fulfilling the prophecy of Zechariah: "Rejoice greatly, O daughter of Zion; shout, O daughter of Jerusalem: behold, thy king cometh unto thee, riding upon an ass, even upon a colt the foal of an ass."[4] It was a pivotal moment in all of their lives—Jesus was at long last signifying that he was the Messiah.

From a true believer's perspective, what happened at Bethphage was not only the dramatic unfolding of God's plan but still another demonstration of Jesus's supernatural powers. Schonfield, however, argued that Jesus had simply prearranged the incident with someone he knew in the vicinity, perhaps Lazarus, and the response "The master needs him" was a code phrase to assure that it was Jesus's disciples who were taking the colt.

Jesus must have realized how the incident would appear to those not in on the secret and that the false perception would work to his benefit, but there was nothing nefarious in what he was doing. He was the instrument of God, and his duty was to fulfill the scriptural prophecies, each of them, as part of a preordained legitimation process for the Messiah.

The most crucial part of the plot Schonfield attributed to Jesus— the part of his thesis that most upset pious Christian readers—was the denouement: the trial, crucifixion, and "resurrection." Schonfield argued that Jesus's expectation was never that he would die on the cross, that since he was absolutely convinced of his calling he had absolute faith that God would not allow his chosen Messiah to die ignobly. His grand design involved contriving a sequence of events in which he would appear to be executed but secretly would survive the ordeal, then be reawakened in a nearby tomb owned by Joseph of Arimathea. Having demonstrated to God his complete trust in him and appearing to the world as someone God had brought back from the dead, Jesus would assume his position on the right hand of the Lord and reign over the chosen people and over the Gentile nations as well.

Two components of the Passover plot were imperative for Jesus: to spend the minimum time possible in agony on the cross and to be administered a drug that would, at the key moment, make him appear lifeless. The former he planned to achieve by orchestrating a hasty trial on the last morning before Passover, expecting to be condemned to execution but also knowing that Jewish law would not permit him to remain on the cross over the Sabbath; hence he would be taken down before sunset that evening. The latter he planned to accomplish by an ingenious ruse. Under the guise of giving him vinegar to drink on the cross, fulfilling yet another prophecy, one of his followers would actually extend to him a sponge soaked in a powerful concoction that would plunge him into a state indistinguishable from death. As soon as that "death" was confirmed, Joseph of Arimathea would request Pontius Pilate's permission to take the body down and place it in his own tomb nearby.

Though daring, it was a well thought out and workable plan. However, for some reason—perhaps the spear plunged into the side of Jesus by a suspicious Roman soldier—it failed. The men entrusted with retrieving him from the tomb found him either near death or already expired and removed him to another location.

The main group of apostles and other followers, who had never been privy to the plot, discovered the empty tomb and were left to interpret the puzzling events as best they could. The two overriding facts were that Jesus had said he would survive death and that all they discovered when they went to the empty tomb were the sheets used to wrap his body. Humiliated by their failure to act when Jesus needed them most, convinced that he had actually been the Messiah, and of course believing his promise that he would be coming back soon to inaugurate the new age, they began to weave the legends that launched the new religion.

For Lennon, whose own cry of the spirit had gone unanswered, this rational and prosaic explanation of Jesus's mission had the ring of authenticity and contributed to his skepticism about organized religion. He took Schonfield's argument to heart, concluding that the increasing secularization he saw in England was due to the public's growing disenchantment (in the pure meaning of the word) with Christianity.

On March 4, 1966, Lennon was interviewed by Maureen Cleave of the London *Evening Standard*. She was one of his favorite reporters, someone with whom he felt no need to be cautious in his comments. During the course of a discussion focused on his life in the suburbs— "How Does a Beatle Live?"—he happened to observe: "Christianity will go. It will vanish and shrink. I needn't argue with that; I'm right and I will be proved right. We're more popular than Jesus now; I don't know which will go first—rock 'n' roll or Christianity. Jesus was all right but his disciples were thick and ordinary. It's them twisting it that ruins it for me."[5]

The comments caused barely a ripple in Britain. They were reported over the next several weeks in *Newsweek*, the *San Francisco Chronicle*, and the *New York Times* without drawing a significant reaction. However, a few months later the interview reappeared in a minor American magazine, *Datebook*. Its editor-publisher made the inflammatory sentence "I don't know which will go first—rock 'n' roll or Christianity" both the headline and a pullout quote and mailed advance copies of the issue to a pair of reactionary disk jockeys in Birmingham, Alabama. They responded as he hoped, trumpeting on the air that John Lennon had declared that the Beatles were more popular than Jesus![6]

Within days a torrent of denunciation erupted from Christian believers living in the "Bible Belt," and the outrage spread rapidly from there. Dozens of radio stations banned Beatles songs from their playlists, and demonstrators tossed their Beatles records into bonfires under the gratified gaze of pastors and deacons.

Lennon was portrayed as a pop star whose mind had been warped by the intense adulation the Beatles enjoyed, someone who now perceived himself to be more important than the Son of God. He even received death threats, which was especially ominous since the Beatles were about to begin a world tour that would culminate in fifteen open-air venues across the United States.

Lennon at first refused to back down from his comments by apologizing for saying something he believed to be true—in effect, by lying for the purpose of keeping Beatles' customers. He preferred to cancel the tour rather than appear to kowtow to those who took offense at what he said. What ultimately changed his mind was recognition of the impact the cancellation would have on his friends in the group. They would be penalized for his outspokenness.

At a press conference in Chicago, the first U.S. stop on the tour, he gave a rambling explanation of the point he had been trying to make in the *Evening Standard* interview: "Well, originally I pointed out that fact in reference to England. That we meant more to kids than Jesus did, or religion at that time. I wasn't knocking it or putting it down. I was just saying it as a fact and it is true more for England than here. I'm not saying that we're better or greater, or comparing us with Jesus Christ as a person or God as a thing or whatever it is. I just said what I said and it was wrong. Or it was taken wrong. And now it's all this."[7]

Finally, after some badgering, the reporters managed to extract from him an apology of sorts: "I still don't know quite what I've done. I've tried to tell you what I did do but if you want me to apologize, if that will make you happy, then OK, I'm sorry."[8]

Officially, the furor ended there, but throughout August there were still threats from the Ku Klux Klan and constant concern about an assassination attempt. The band's greatest worry was the performance in Memphis. Their hearts jumped that night when in the middle of the concert they heard an explosion on stage. But the momentary scare was merely someone tossing a firecracker into their midst.[9] When the harrowing tour came to an end at Candlestick Park in San Francisco, the Beatles agreed that they would never tour again.

While Lennon continued to use the word *God* regularly in conversation, he never, after reading *The Passover Plot*, accepted the notion that there is a deity somewhere who takes an interest in human affairs. For him the term was shorthand to connote some indefinable force within nature, a force he sometimes called magic, that lay at the heart of the religious/spiritual sentiment. Reflecting back over his career and life in a *Playboy* interview shortly before his death, he said: "People got the image I was anti-Christ or antireligion. I'm not at all. I'm a most religious fellow. . . . I'm certainly not an atheist. There is more that we still could know. I think this magic is just a way of saying science we don't know yet or we haven't explored yet. That's not antireligious at all."[10]

He elaborated on the same theme on another occasion: "I don't know that anyone like me, who questions everything down to the colour of his socks, can believe in an old man in the sky." Then, after a thoughtful silence: "I believe in something, definitely. I believe there is a force at work that you can't physically account for."[11]

When someone posed the question to him very straightforwardly, "Do you believe in God?" he responded by being more specific, offering a very potent and suggestive simile: "Yes. I believe that God is like a powerhouse, like where you keep electricity, like a power station. And that he's a supreme power, and that he's neither good nor bad, left, right, black or white. He just is. And we tap that source of power and make of it what we will. Just as electricity can kill people in a chair, or you can light the room with it."[12]

The powerhouse simile made more understandable his comments in another interview in which he voiced his feeling that he and Paul were not the creators of, but merely the channels for, the songs they wrote. Then he digressed: "It's like when you talk about God, you know. I say 'God,' I mean 'God,' I mean 'Goddess,' I mean 'It.' . . . But when I refer to God in private, I don't have to go 'God,' 'Gods,' 'Goddesses,' 'It.' You know, like, Yoko, or whoever I'm talking to, understands that I'm talking about 'It' more than One Old Man in the Sky."[13]

Lennon came to hold the view that a personified God was a defense mechanism of the human brain confronted by the stresses of life. In his song "God," he concisely expresses this point of view with an aphorism: "God is a concept by which we measure our pain."

The song, written when he was turning thirty, could be considered Lennon's declaration of independence. After beginning with the aphorism, he offers a litany of subjects in which he declares he does not believe, among them Jesus, Buddha, the Bible, and the Bhagavad Gita. He also includes Kennedy, Elvis, and Zimmerman (Bob Dylan) in the list, and culminates with the Beatles. His objective is quite straightforward: to stand alone intellectually—rejecting *all* belief systems and *all* idols, even the idol he had helped to create and to which he owed his power and influence.

After rejection of all the accumulated reasoning and opinion, logic and revelation, surmise and speculation, wisdom and tommyrot of other well-meaning but fallible people, what remains?

A free-thinking, self-directing individual.

Descartes had proposed as an axiom: "I think, therefore I am." Lennon's version might have been phrased: "I don't believe, therefore I am."

Following the string of negatives in "God," Lennon concludes positively, declaring a reality that is all his own. No longer willing to be enchanted by ancient texts and famous figures, he shifts his focus to the here and now. The foundation of his reality will be what he experiences himself and his relationship with the woman he loves.

With the exception of his brief association with the Maharishi Mahesh Yogi, Lennon never exhibited a desire to belong to a larger spiritual group. As he once responded to a question about whether he and Yoko Ono were Buddhists, "No. No, I'm nothing. No, no, no label. You can call me a Zen Christian, a Zen Pagan. A Zen Marxist. . . . I don't belong to anything."[14]

While rejecting organized religion, Lennon reserved judgment about the possibility that the individual personality or spirit could survive physical death. Paul McCartney acknowledged that the Beatles had discussed life after death and all four had pledged that the one who died first would try to communicate with the others. Lennon also promised his son Julian that if anything happened to him he would send a sign to verify he was all right—a feather would appear to him in a closed room and drift down to the floor. Neither the pact nor the promise was fulfilled after Lennon's death.[15]

By the time "God" was written, late in 1970, Lennon had for several years been a godlike figure himself. As the intellectual leader of the group in the vanguard of creating culture for the wave of youth born after World War II, he could count on his opinions and judgments being disseminated around the planet.

He tried to use the tool to good effect, consciously propagating a message of peace and love; but while his ego undoubtedly savored the experience of being a deity, he grew increasingly dissatisfied in the role. Those who were trying to shape public opinion for a cause knew that just the *appearance* of having John Lennon's support would create momentum, so they continually struggled to gain his ear and used every tool of persuasion imaginable to engage him in their own agendas.

In another song written at about the same time as "God," he revealed his disgust with their machinations ("Don't give me that brother, brother . . .") and his distress with human self-deception—religious beliefs in particular. "I Found Out" employs lyrics that are deliberately nonpoetic, stripped of all artifice, to express what Lennon had concluded from his own search and to encourage others to follow his lead in shaking off culturally acquired belief systems.

His message is blunt: stop accepting what you've been told; assert your independence and individuality; don't be mentally shackled by rules that someone else devised.

Once fooled himself, he warns others about searching for a guru. Why defer to the belief system of some "holy man" when he has no way to appreciate or value your individual life experiences, perceptions, and potential? Don't count on Jesus to come back and save you, he says. As for those who chant "Hare Krishna" all day, that just keeps their minds focused on "pie in the sky" and distracted from the real world.

Nor are drugs an answer. They are only a diversion, not any sort of solution or defense. Others cannot harm us (psychologically) unless we accept that they have the authority to do so. We should deny them that authority and feel free to experience our own lives—even the inevitable pain that occurs.

His overall point in "I Found Out" is not to place anyone above you. Don't allow yourself to become a follower and in doing so devalue your own life experiences and insights. Keep your own unique perspective as an individual, even if it means you have to suffer without the solace of a personalized deity.

Lennon's brusque language and abrasive attitude, which may have been a residual effect of the Primal Scream therapy he had recently completed, is guaranteed to antagonize many listeners. Some critics might even dismiss his body blows against religion as simply another exhibition of the antiauthority position he had developed as a conflicted teenager and then taken into adulthood.

However, from another point of view, perhaps he felt that body blows were necessary. How many adults ever sincerely question the religious indoctrination they received as children? How many of us ever emerge from the fog of *any* of our strongly held beliefs and look back at them objectively? Besides, the sharpness of his attack is blunted by other comments Lennon made in interviews. Recall his statement in another context, "People got the image I was anti-Christ or antireligion. I'm not at all. . . . I'm certainly not an atheist."

His tirade in "I Found Out" was directed at the dogma of religions and the deification of the great personalities who had inspired them, not the moral and ethical principles put forward by those personalities. The harshness in his voice reflected his anger at the way religions too often come to dominate the lives of their adherents instead of uplifting them through the wisdom of their founders.

Years before, Lennon had expressed similar harshness in print, but in such obscure language that few could grasp his meaning. In *A Spaniard in the Works*, his second book, he offered a number of barbed references to Christianity. Many readers of this book, as well as of his first, *In His Own Write*, assumed that he was writing nonsense in the same vein as Lewis Carroll in his classic poem "Jabberwocky." Critics who were familiar with

James Joyce's *Finnegan's Wake*, however, realized that transpiring beneath the whimsical surface was something more significant.

All of which is not to say that Lennon didn't take pleasure in dashing off nonsense—he greatly admired Carroll and Edward Lear—but he also had a passion for parody and satire. Like James Joyce, he developed an idiosyncratic writing style that combined sophisticated punning, splicing of words, bizarre (but usually meaningful) orthography, and inside jokes, and he employed the technique to convey the flow of a story while simultaneously revealing more information about it—especially critical comments.

One of the poems in *A Spaniard in the Works* provides an excellent case in point. In "The Faulty Bagnose," every stanza contains allusions that would affront believers (in this case, adherents of the Anglican Church); but these references are always so encrypted in "Lennonese" that most such readers would not catch them, and those who did would find it difficult to make a convincing argument to someone who was skeptical of their suspicions.

What, for example, are we to make of the central figure in the poem, the "Mungle"? And what hidden meaning lurks behind such language as "The Mungle pilgriffs far awoy Religeorge too thee world"?

Dr. James Sauceda, a scholar who wrote his doctoral dissertation on *Finnegan's Wake*, conducted an exhaustive study of Lennon's literary work. His summation of the key theme of "The Faulty Bagnose" is, "Christianity viewed as a harshly judgmental, hypocritical, and virtually incoherent belief system." The meaning he derives from the linguistically encrypted "faulty bagnose" is "the fault finding and faulty bag of noise." "Mungle," it turns out, is a real word. The meaning is "a stick for stirring"—which Sauceda equates with a preacher leading the congregation. He interprets "pilgriffs" as the Pilgrims who went far away ("awoy" hinting at the nautical "Ahoy!"), trying to escape the religious persecution of George III ("Reli*george*").[16] Lennon appears to be saying in this poem, in his own highly inventive way, that he and the other Beatles no longer want to associate themselves with the flawed and corrupt religion of the establishment.

After Lennon rejected the Christianity in which he had been raised and organized religion in general, his approach to life became secular and humanistic. Whatever problems we have on this planet, he seemed to conclude, we have nowhere else to turn for solutions. We need to clear our minds and act together to solve them.

5

LOVE

The same winter John Lennon made his unanswered appeal to God and read and was assimilating *The Passover Plot*, he began to take lysergic acid diethylamide (LSD) on a regular basis. In it he discovered a substitute religious experience, one that would have a transforming effect on his personality and a liberating effect on his music.

His first encounter with the drug had taken place over a year earlier when the Beatles were filming *Help!* He and Cynthia accompanied George Harrison and his girlfriend, Pattie Boyd, to a dinner at the home of Harrison's dentist in London. Afterward, as they were having coffee, their host, without telling them the significance, dropped sugar cubes into their cups. Soon they all began to experience distorted perceptions—furniture seemed to change shape, the room appeared vast, colors became alarmingly vibrant, time stopped. They all panicked and determined to flee. Their host tried to dissuade them, knowing they were about to have mental experiences for which none of them would be prepared. He admitted that the sugar cubes had been laced with LSD, but his frantic appeals terrified the women. They imagined that the drug had aphrodisiac effects and feared that what the man had in mind was an orgy.

Rather than return home, however, they continued on to the Pickwick Club, their planned next stop. They stayed only a few minutes, unnerved by the staring crowd and the phantasmagorical effects of the drug. They proceeded to the Ad Lib, a club they knew better, hoping the familiar surroundings would help them deal with the experience. When they arrived at the building they were amazed at the illumination and thought a premiere must be in progress. Actually, it was the normal lighting. In the elevator, a red light on the control panel caught their attention; they all began to fixate on it and panicked, having the illusion that the elevator was on fire. When they arrived at their floor they were screaming. Unable to cope with their heightened perceptions, they again stayed only briefly.

Harrison, despite having all of his senses distorted, somehow managed to drive them slowly back to his home, where they spent the next several hours hallucinating. While the others retreated to the seclusion of upstairs bedrooms, Lennon stayed downstairs alone and began to draw. Later he had the vivid hallucination that Harrison's house was a huge submarine on which he had to remain at the helm to steer.[1]

After the initial terror of the incident wore off and he could look back on it objectively, Lennon became fascinated by the distortion of his perceptions, which introduced a new element of excitement into his life. He sampled LSD again that August when the Beatles stopped in Los Angeles on their 1965 tour.

He had already been reading *The Doors of Perception* by Aldous Huxley, which dealt with Huxley's experiences with mescaline and was extremely popular around that time.[2] At some point that winter he picked up and read *The Psychedelic Experience* by Timothy Leary, Ralph Metzner, and Richard Alpert. All Ph.D.'s, they had undertaken a series of controversial experiments at Harvard University to investigate the effects of psychedelic stimulants on themselves and student volunteers, and the book was written as a manual on how to conduct such experimentation outside an academic setting.

What made the manual especially intriguing was that in form, content, and even nomenclature it was modeled on *The Tibetan Book of the Dead*. The three researchers had discovered that the psychoneural territory they had been mapping out in their experiments was already well covered in the 2,500-year-old text, only characterized differently—as stages of the "postdeath" experience. They therefore contended that beneath what was exoterically a guide to the period between death and rebirth hid an esoteric message. The ancient book was actually intended to steer new initiates through higher levels of consciousness.

When, ultimately, Lennon found a source of LSD in England, he became a regular user and undertook his own explorations, welcoming the drug's impact on both his spiritual quest and his creativity. Cynthia Lennon, who compared her first LSD trip with being trapped in a nightmare, could not understand her husband's fascination with the drug, but in her book about their years together she candidly admitted the benefits it held for him. "It was like living with someone who had just discovered religion. . . . In many ways it was a wonderful thing to watch. Tensions, bigotry, and bad temper were replaced by understanding and love."[3]

In addition to the psychological changes, Lennon became a vegetarian and lost the weight that had been making him feel fat and awkward. (Pete Shotton recalled Lennon's conviction that Jesus must have been a vegetarian too and his scouring the New Testament for clues.)[4] On the negative side, his use of the substance resulted in growing alienation from his wife, since she never learned to enjoy its effect and refused to keep him company on his acid trips.

The use of drugs to enhance creativity had a long history in England, going back at least to the days of Samuel Taylor Coleridge and Thomas De Quincey. But Lennon's use of LSD must also be seen in the context of his own time. During the mid-1960s, on both sides of the Atlantic, the children of the baby boom were coming to maturity. Because they constituted an unusually large percentage of the population, the natural openness of their age group toward questioning values and taking idealistic positions carried added weight in society. From minor issues such as hair length for men and skirt length for women to larger concerns such as social mores, sexual freedom, gender roles, race relations, economic inequities, and support for the government in wartime—all that had been taken for granted up to their day was considered fair game for reevaluation and change.

The self-reinforcing energy of the "youthquake" led to widespread speculation and belief that a new stage of consciousness was developing, a leap forward by the species, with the Western nations leading the way—

a transformation that would coincide with the supposed dawning of the Age of Aquarius. It would be an age characterized by social harmony and the spread of love and understanding.

Timothy Leary and his coauthors contributed to that belief in *The Psychedelic Experience*. They argued that, if used properly, chemicals such as LSD, mescaline, and psilocybin could accelerate the understanding and embrace of the new consciousness. The key, and the goal, was to extinguish the ego and eliminate our perceived duality with the universe, to recognize that we are just temporary aggregations of energy localized in a continuous and infinite ocean of energy and that the world of discrete matter we perceive is just a useful illusion.

Lennon, adventurous in spirit, desperate to discover something that would give his life meaning, plunged into the New Age with abandon. In an interview with *Rolling Stone* in late 1970, he stated that he had easily taken a thousand LSD trips.[5]

Lennon found that lysergic acid also had a positive effect on his creativity. His first validation was "Tomorrow Never Knows," recorded in April 1966. The song was breathtakingly original—like a leap across a chasm into some musical realm where Salvador Dali had designed all the instruments. Eerie noises and rhythms erupted and tailed off, orchestrated by intuition, twisting like a whirlwind around Lennon's seemingly disembodied voice. He based his lyrics on the concepts and language in *The Psychedelic Experience* and *The Tibetan Book of the Dead*. In fact, his original conception involved singing the lyrics against a background of thousands of monks chanting.

"Rain" followed, recorded just a week later, its lyrics asserting that reality is just a state of mind. Not content with the sounds of musical instruments being played in reverse, Lennon even sang words backward. "She Said, She Said" was inspired directly by the acid trip he had taken a year earlier in Los Angeles in the company of actor Peter Fonda.

"Strawberry Fields Forever," which he first conceived as a gentle, lyrical introspection, became, through the influence of LSD, immense and enigmatic. The finished song conveys the impression of Lennon walking in slow motion through a grand architecture of sound inspired by Lewis

Carroll, confiding revelations from his subconscious. He always rated it as one of his finest songs and among his most personal.

The two most impressive LSD-inspired songs Lennon wrote both appeared on the classic album *Sgt. Pepper's Lonely Hearts Club Band*. The first even had the three letters LSD imbedded into the title as the initial letters of the key words. Lennon always maintained that it was coincidence, that his son Julian had come home from school one day carrying a drawing he had made—a woman riding a horse across the sky surrounded by exploding stars. When he asked Julian what he called the drawing, he replied, "Lucy in the sky with diamonds."

Lennon so loved the phrase that he wrote a song around it. He imagined a tumbling stream of phantasmagorical images like those from *Alice in Wonderland* but also suggestive of an acid trip. Only later, when someone pointed it out to him, did he see and appreciate the coincidence in the title. That it really was coincidence was corroborated by Pete Shotton, who happened to be with Lennon when Julian showed him the drawing.[6] It is not too difficult to imagine how the coincidence came about. As a regular user of LSD, Lennon undoubtedly referred to it within Julian's hearing, probably on multiple occasions. A clever four-year-old would likely wonder what the letters spelled, and by playing with them mentally might invent a fanciful phrase and then create a drawing based on it.

The second LSD-influenced song on *Sgt. Pepper* was so creative and so powerful that it became the capstone of the most highly praised album the Beatles ever recorded. "A Day in the Life" encapsulates the absurdity of postmodern existence: the crowd around a corpse speculates about its social class; a man sits through a boring movie just to see how it compares with the book; diligent hole counters fan out across a busy town to come up with an accurate number.

Much of the song's inspiration came straight from the newspaper. The traffic accident mentioned happened on December 18, 1966, and Lennon read about it the next day in the *Daily Mail*. The dead driver of the car was well known to the group—twenty-one-year-old Tara Browne, heir to the Guinness fortune.[7] In the very same newspaper Lennon found an article reporting the asinine "fact" that four thousand potholes had been tallied in Blackburn, Lancashire. The film referred to was almost certainly an allusion to *How I Won the War*, the antiwar movie Lennon had appeared in the previous fall.

Very deftly, Lennon wove the unrelated images into a comment on the precariousness and inanity of life and capped it all with the wonderfully absurd observation about how many holes it takes to fill the Albert Hall. His point was delivered as a gentle invitation to "turn on" (suggested by McCartney, who added lyrics about waking up and catching a bus), inserted just prior to an orchestral passage that went soaring into the stratosphere. Yes, he was saying, our existence is absurd, but we can rise above it by expanding our consciousness. We can achieve a state in which we are able to dismiss the mundane and ridiculous and focus on what is important. And psychedelic drugs are the shortcut to expanded consciousness.

But just what *was* important in Lennon's eyes?

Ever since "The Word" in late 1965, a tune written to acknowledge his mellowed attitude as a result of smoking marijuana, Lennon had propounded a message that, depending on the state of mind of the listener, was either remarkably naive or refreshingly idealistic. "The Word" was *love*. As someone who had never received it from his father, only sporadically from his mother, and with great reserve by his de facto mother, Mimi, Lennon was acutely sensitized to its importance in human psychology and in social relations. Through his self-explorations under the influence of marijuana and LSD, he grasped the elemental truth even more clearly. If all could maintain love in their hearts for everyone else—and for the world in general—all problems and strife would resolve.

He was unambiguous about his intention; he openly declared that he wanted to show everybody the light. Because of their exalted position, the Beatles were in the position to influence minds, particularly those of the young, and Lennon came to see it not just as an opportunity but as their *responsibility* to make a positive contribution. Just as Viktor E. Frankl had proposed, Lennon had come to realize that responsibility brought meaning into his pointless existence. Which life did he find more satisfying—that of a pop star indulging himself or of a therapist committed to improving the world?

An unprecedented opportunity arose in mid-1967. The matrix of satellites being used to transmit television signals internationally had reached a stage where a program could be broadcast simultaneously in every corner of the planet. To mark the occasion, a number of nations agreed to collaborate in the production of a single program called *Our World*, which would be the first ever viewed live by a global audience. Each nation was invited to choose the appropriate entertainment for its segment. The British government, in acknowledgment of the Beatles' universal popularity, asked them to represent the United Kingdom.

Rather than simply perform a song from their repertory, they proposed to come up with a new song and record it live during the broadcast. Lennon and Paul McCartney entered into a friendly competition to write one significant enough for the occasion, wanting to capitalize on the opportunity presented to deliver a message to the largest audience in history. Lennon responded to the challenge by writing an anthem.

An estimated four hundred million people witnessed the debut of "All You Need Is Love."[8] The language used in the song was so simple that even viewers with only a rudimentary grasp of English could understand Lennon's message.

While the concept expressed seems trite on its surface, it was no more so than Albert Schweitzer's "reverence for life" or Jesus's "Do unto others as you would have them do unto you." What Lennon did, with mantralike repetition, was to spread the hippie message of the mid-sixties: society was a mess and needed to be redirected. However, Lennon claimed, paradoxically, that the solution did not lie in striving to change society but in striving to change oneself. *Outward*-directed efforts might be commendable, but the transformation was needed *inside*.

Through engagement with the world you risked entanglement and defeat, and even if successful you achieved nothing that someone else couldn't achieve. The one thing you could do that absolutely no one else could do was to change yourself—to "learn how to be you in time." The mechanism was love, and by allowing it to manifest through your actions you could positively affect the people around you, and they others, and, as the ripples continued to spread outward, everyone everywhere.

Still only twenty-six, Lennon had not been drained of the optimism of youth. Perhaps the world *could* be changed. Perhaps a chain reaction *could* be achieved if one reached and motivated a critical mass of listeners—and an audience of several hundred million provided a significant start.

By the time he turned thirty, that optimism had been tempered. Responding to a post-Beatles question about the group's impact on history, he said:

> The people who are in control and in power and the class system and the whole bullshit bourgeois scene is exactly the same. . . . We've grown up a little, all of us, and there has been a change and we are a bit freer and all that, but it's the same game. Nothing's really changed. It's the *same*! . . . They're doing exactly the same things, selling arms to South Africa, killing blacks in the streets. . . . It just makes you puke, and I woke up to that, too. That dream is over, it's just the same, only I'm thirty and a lot of people have got long hair, that's all.[9]

Notwithstanding his later disillusionment, the message of Lennon's 1967 song had a timeless validity that could not be tarnished even if the scope of its impact was less than he hoped—just as the messages of Jesus and Schweitzer continue to resonate with, inspire, and motivate some but not all of humanity.

This message—love—was so universal that it superseded any impulse to recommend the use of chemicals, and, in fact, by the time "All You Need Is Love" was released as a record, Lennon's fascination with LSD had worn thin. Although it had been beneficial in his own transformation, he still had had many bad trips on LSD. Then, in early August, George Harrison informed him that he was discontinuing use of the substance. He had visited the Haight-Ashbury district in San Francisco expecting to see love in action and instead his eyes had been opened to the tragic impact drugs had on most people's lives. At about that same time, Lennon received a letter from a friend who warned him that lysergic acid could permanently alter the organization of his brain, and he came to a realization: he had already explored all the byways of that street, why continue down it?

As *The Psychedelic Experience* had revealed, drugs could serve as a short-cut to higher levels of consciousness. But the levels themselves were already there. They had been explored millennia before by inquisitive people who employed other means to reach them. The monks of Tibet were not unique; ascetics in other ancient lands had discovered the same esoteric knowledge through similar methods. For thousands of years, enlightened individuals had acted as teachers to other seekers, passing knowledge of the higher levels along—and the time-tested process for achieving them involved meditation.

6

MEDITATION

John Lennon's introduction to meditation was the result of a chain of events that began during the filming of *Help!* To add spice to one scene, the director called in a group of Indian musicians to play while the action took place around them, and later a twenty-one-string sitar was used for effect on instrumental tracks of the soundtrack album.[1]

When George Harrison heard the sound of the Indian instruments, he became enthralled. He bought a sitar and used it to create an exotic atmosphere for Lennon's song "Norwegian Wood," though not playing it in the way it was meant to be played. When the best-known master of sitar, Ravi Shankar, traveled to London, Harrison met him at a dinner party. The pop superstar confided his desire to learn the complex instrument, and Shankar responded by inviting him to stay at Shankar's home in Bombay, where he could study it in depth.[2]

Harrison traveled to India in October 1966, taking along his new wife, the former Pattie Boyd. She shared her husband's fascination with the country and its ancient culture, and after their return to England she became intrigued by the Spiritual Regeneration Movement and its leader, Maharishi Mahesh Yogi.[3]

In February 1967, she attended a lecture on the Maharishi's technique for achieving rapid and deep meditation. She immediately became a practitioner and received initiation and a mantra. Her enthusiasm influenced her husband and Lennon, among others, to open their minds to the benefits of the method. Lennon joined the organization and received instruction and his mantra. He became diligent about meditating daily. [4]

Thus they were all excited to learn that the Maharishi, the charismatic founder of the movement and chief expert on the method, had decided to come to London to lecture. By a curious coincidence of history, it was to be the last such public lecture the Maharishi would ever give.[5]

On the evening of Friday, August 24, 1967, Lennon and Harrison with their wives and McCartney with his girlfriend, Jane Asher, all arrived at London's Park Lane Hilton to listen to the Maharishi expound on his message.[6] Their expectations were high. Since they had already begun to see the benefits of the method, the man who had brought it to the world's attention must be a personage worth meeting. More promising still, he carried the imposing title of Yogi.

They were all familiar with *The Autobiography of a Yogi*, which relates the life of Paramahansa Yogananda, an Indian sage who lived in the West for many years and popularized yoga.[7] Among other colorful events, the book describes amazing feats Yogis are able to perform as a result of their physical and spiritual training. These include clairvoyance, levitation, existing for years without eating or drinking, and simultaneous materialization of the body at other locations. Since the Maharishi called himself a Yogi, the Beatles obviously had hopes that he would give a demonstration of such powers—and undoubtedly harbored secret fantasies that he would teach them how to perform the feats.

The fifty-year-old Maharishi turned out to be a curious little figure with untamed long hair and beard who kept subverting his holy-man image by a tendency to giggle and laugh. That ultimately added to his appeal, however, since his irrepressible cheerfulness seemed to flow from some inner light.

His message was simple. Everywhere he looked he saw people discontented and unhappy. The world needed spiritual regeneration, and that was his goal. But it was not necessary for everyone to do as he had done—renounce society and live in a cave in the Himalayas for years. People could take active control of their existence and regenerate themselves spiritually while carrying on with their present lives.

They could do so by practicing a simple and easy meditation technique his own guru had taught him years before. The daily performance of this technique would transform them from within, and after a few sessions they would feel radiant with happiness and help spread a wave of peace and love across the world.

Lennon could not have heard a lecture that more echoed his ambitions at the time. Ever since the simultaneous and paradoxical arrival of success and meaninglessness in his life, he had struggled to escape despair by discovering his own mission and using his influence as a Beatle to disseminate his message. The one message that seemed a valid use of his time and commitment was the spread of love and peace, to be achieved through self-transformation. Now the Maharishi was saying precisely the same thing, with the added benefit of a proven technique to carry out the agenda.

What made the development even more welcome was that the Maharishi made no effort to impose a religious doctrine. He had his own, derived from ancient Indian texts, but he kept it separate from his mission to teach the world his meditation technique. The method could be used by anyone, regardless of background or belief system. If one would simply set aside time to practice it daily in the prescribed manner, he or she would benefit, and the rest of the world would also benefit. End of sermon.

After the lecture the Beatles were invited up to the Maharishi's hotel suite, and in the course of that conversation he invited them to come to a special retreat he was hosting in Bangor in northern Wales.[8] Though they would have to leave the very next day, they were all so enthusiastic about what he represented that they dropped other plans and prepared to accompany him. The holy man insisted on one condition: they would have to forgo drugs.

The next day they caught the train to Bangor. Upon arrival, they settled into the spartan accommodations, a college dormitory, and on Saturday morning held a press conference in which they described their interest in the Maharishi's teachings and announced they had given up drugs.

They no sooner began to receive personal instruction from the Maharishi than they had their first confirmation of his cosmic perspective. Word reached them on Sunday afternoon that Brian Epstein had died suddenly at the age of thirty-two of unknown causes that had the earmarks of an accidental drug overdose.

The Maharishi invited them into his chamber to discuss the news. They found him surrounded by a magnificent arrangement of flowers, and he surprised them by reacting cheerfully. He advised them to be happy, not sad. There was no death, only transition, and the painful vibrations they were sending out would hinder Epstein's journey to the next world. They should be joyful. Then their friend's spirit would be joyful, too.[9]

Whatever the wisdom in his advice, the Beatles suffered widespread criticism when they emerged from the room smiling and laughing to be interviewed by the waiting media. The man who had been instrumental in launching them to worldwide fame and great fortune—a close personal friend—had died at a tragically young age, and they seemed to be enjoying their day.

Pete Shotton visited Lennon the next morning on his return to Weybridge. He immediately brought up the subject, and Lennon restated the Maharishi's position: "It is bad news. But it's up to us now to just think happy thoughts about Brian; then he'll be OK. The Maharishi told us that death is just an illusion, and we mustn't get depressed about it or feel sorry for ourselves. We've all got to try to think about Brian in a positive way, to help him get wherever it is he should be going."[10]

Lennon continued to practice daily meditation for the next several months and expressed support for the Maharishi and his goals in interviews. Given his own conclusions about religion, he could not have done so had the movement been sectarian, but the Maharishi always stressed that all he was promoting was a natural and scientific technique: "So this [meditation] is useful to man to develop his individuality and then the fully developed man will find his God through his religion. Christians will realize God through Christianity, Muslims will realize God through Islam. But they will become fully developed Christians and fully developed Muslims and fully developed Hindus. So this we say is a technique and not a religion. Useful to the people of all religions."[11]

Lennon made a similar point succinctly in an interview: "It's nothing to do with mysticism. It's about *understanding*."[12]

In early 1968, Lennon and the other three Beatles prepared to take part in a more extended retreat at the Maharishi's spiritual headquarters in northern India, a remote ashram situated on the banks of the sacred Ganges River. Away from the distractions of the world they knew, they would be free to devote themselves to meditation and have the benefit of private daily instruction from the master.

Just days before departing they recorded Lennon's "Across the Universe," in which he expresses his newfound serenity under the Maharishi's guidance. In a touch of what might be irony or perhaps meaningful juxtaposition or only whimsy, he opens the song with a guitar lead-in that echoes the melody from "Nowhere Man." Then he offers poetic glimpses of the experience of deep meditation.

Lennon also incorporates, with the feeling of a mantra, a tribute to the teacher the Maharishi revered: "*Jai Guru Deva Om.*" The Maharishi encouraged the use of the Sanskrit phrase *Jai Guru Dev* among members of his organization as a way to recognize and honor his mentor, Swami Brahmananda, or as many of his disciples called him, "Guru Dev"— *dev* or *deva* being Sanskrit for "divine." Translated, the phrase in Lennon's song means "Hail the Divine Guru," with the added *Om* being the sacred word in Sanskrit often used as a mantra itself.[13]

Anchoring the song is a contented, haunting refrain in which he assures us that nothing will change his world. Lennon was convinced that his search had ended. He had found his mission in life. In his enthusiasm, he proposed that the Beatles take an instrumental role in the spread of the Maharishi's message, giving financial backing for a worldwide network of retreats and training centers. He even suggested to the other three that the group serve as the holy man's apostles: "If we went round the world preaching about transcendental meditation, we could turn on millions of people."[14]

When the Beatles arrived at the ashram of Rishikesh in February 1968, they were the most luminous in a star-filled assemblage that included singers-songwriters Mike Love of the Beach Boys and Donovan Leitch and actress Mia Farrow. Lennon was respectful of the Yogi but not in awe. Donovan told the story of how, when the visitors first arrived, everyone gathered in a room around the impressive Maharishi, who was sitting cross-legged on the floor, appearing amiable but nontalkative. An awkward silence developed. No one knew what to say around him. Lennon broke the ice by striding across the room and patting the diminutive holy man on top of the head. "There's a good little guru," he said, provoking an eruption of laughter.[15]

After some initial harassment by reporters seeking to find out what was happening at the ashram, the devotees were left in peace to meditate and study. With the exception of a few conveniences the Maharishi had arranged for his famous disciples, they lived a simple existence, sleeping in stone bungalows and taking vegetarian meals communally outdoors. They were lectured each day by the Maharishi and were free to pose questions about their experiences while meditating, but as the weeks went by they were encouraged to spend longer and longer periods in silent meditation in their rooms.

In essence, the Maharishi taught that there were seven levels of consciousness.[16] The first three were waking, dreaming, and deep sleep. The fourth, which could be reached through meditation, he described as transcendental and labeled "pure consciousness." After reaching this state, a person who meditated diligently could get beyond the thought process entirely and become aware of a fifth state in which the Absolute—or Being itself—was experienced, a state the Maharishi called "cosmic consciousness." Having reached it, the individual would be able to maintain awareness of Being even while going about his or her daily life. Higher still were levels the Maharishi called God consciousness and Supreme Knowledge, which were difficult to grasp and difficult to speak about.

He later said of God consciousness: "In this further development, the liveliness of the infinite is cognized on the bed of the finite. This is only possible when the conscious mind has become vibrant with the infinite value and the perception has become so refined as to spontaneously cognize the finest relative values. In this situation, the finest relative perception rises to the level of the infinite value of perception."[17]

Of the seventh and highest state, which he declared his own teacher, Guru Dev, had attained, he later said: "In this unified state of consciousness, the experiencer and the object of experience have both been brought to the same level of infinite value, and this encompasses the entire phenomenon of perception and action as well. The gulf between the knower and the object of his knowing has been bridged."[18]

According to the Maharishi, these levels were real and attainable by all depending upon their commitment to meditation and to purifying themselves. He maintained that they could be studied scientifically, and he spoke as someone with a scientifically oriented brain himself, having earned degrees in physics and mathematics from Allahabad University.

Did Lennon understand and agree with everything his guru taught? He was at least willing to commit his time and energy to finding out how much was true. He and George Harrison were the most dedicated pupils among the celebrities, sitting for up to eight or nine hours a day, striving to harmonize themselves with the elusive states.[19]

As time went on, however, there was growing dissonance in Eden. Lennon was perfectly willing to hurl himself down the road the Maharishi had indicated, but he expected to see results. According to Neil Aspinall, an aide to the Beatles, "John thought there was some sort of secret the Maharishi had to give you, and then you could just go home. He started to think the Maharishi was holding out on him." The Maharishi kept a helicopter at the site, which he used to facilitate travel from the remote ashram. Lennon speculated mischievously that if he could just get the holy man to take him up for a ride, away from the others, perhaps he would slip him the secret on his own.[20]

Aspinall began to suspect that there was more to the simple little guru than anyone knew when he was assigned to negotiate with the Maharishi about creating a film in which the guru would star. "We had a meeting about it in his bungalow. Suddenly, this little guy in a robe who's meant to be a Holy man starts talking about his two and a half percent. 'Wait a minute,' I thought, 'He knows more about making deals than I do. He's really into scoring, the Maharishi.'"[21]

Several weeks into the retreat, Alex Mardas, a friend of Lennon's, arrived. He was immediately skeptical of some of the accommodations the Maharishi had provided for his celebrity guests. "An ashram with four-poster beds?" he demanded incredulously. "Masseurs, and servants bringing water, houses with facilities, an accountant—I never saw a holy man with a bookkeeper!"[22]

More troubling still, Mardas befriended a blonde nurse from California who confided in him that on five different occasions she had had sexual relations with the supposedly celibate master. Mardas reported the allegations to the others, which sent emotions raging through the Beatles' circle, with some ready to believe the worst, others defending the guru's integrity. Cynthia Lennon suspected Mardas more than the Maharishi. She believed that he was jealous about the guru's influence over her husband. Lennon and Harrison also found the charge unthinkable and debated the issue throughout a long night.

Suspicions inflamed each other. Why had Mia Farrow seemed to get preferential consideration—being lodged adjacent to the Maharishi? For that matter, why had she abruptly left the retreat early? What about the Maharishi's deal-making expertise? And why did a simple and unpretentious holy man need a helicopter at his disposal?

Then they began to recall earlier incidents, such as one the previous fall when they learned the Maharishi had assured third parties the Beatles would endorse and take part in events they had specifically told him they would not. It began to gnaw at Lennon that, as much as he thought of himself as cynical and worldly-wise, in his desire to commit himself to an important cause he might have been played for a fool.

Lennon, Harrison, and Mardas went together to confront the Maharishi. Lennon was abrupt. "We're leaving."

"Why?" the guru asked.

They had heard intimations about the Maharishi's supernatural abilities from his followers but had never seen any proof themselves. Lennon openly challenged him to display them: "Well, if you're so cosmic, you'll know why."

Nothing supernatural was forthcoming. The guru responded to the acid comment, "I don't know why, you must tell me."

Lennon later said of that tense encounter: "And I just kept saying 'You know why'—and he gave me a look like, 'I'll kill you, you bastard.' He gave me such a look, and I knew then when he looked at me, because I'd called his bluff. And I was a bit rough to him."[23]

They packed their bags and, while they were waiting for Mardas to return from Rishikesh with cars to take them back to civilization, Lennon sat down and wrote a song blasting the Maharishi. ("You've made a fool of everyone.") Two months intervened before he would record it. During that time he thought better about directly naming the subject of his attack. The Maharishi changed gender and became "Sexy Sadie."

No one ever ascertained whether the nurse's allegations were true. Both Cynthia Lennon and George Harrison later believed that the whole scene was concocted by Alex Mardas to discredit the Maharishi in order to free Lennon from his grip. But Lennon gave the greatest weight to the murderous look he had seen in the guru's eyes. His intuitive flash seemed vindicated later when further allegations came out from one of the Maharishi's leading female disciples.[24] Mia Farrow would also confirm in her autobiography that her abrupt departure from the ashram had been prompted by the guru's groping her during a meditation session in his private "cave."[25]

However great his disappointment and disenchantment with the Maharishi, Lennon benefited from the experience by receiving instruction in meditation from a master. For the rest of his life, he often turned to meditation to restore himself and improve his creativity. He characterized his use of it as "mysticism," but not in a supernatural or religious sense, as poet and Zen devotee Allen Ginsberg learned from a discussion he had with Lennon in 1971: "I told him I thought that meditation practice was a good idea. John asked me if I believed in God. I said yes. He challenged me on that. My meditation at that time was, alas, somewhat theistic—schmaltzy, sentimental. He was nontheistic, which was pretty smart; he was ahead of me there. So it was hard for me to defend meditation practice itself, when my own idea of it was based on a theistic premise that John had rightly seen as baseless."[26]

Instead, Lennon's view of the practice of meditation was pragmatic. He wrote of it, in 1978, as a way to slip out of the "straitjacket" of the mind. He characterized it as a source of creative inspiration. In order to create, one must first empty the mind: "You can't paint a picture on dirty paper; you need a clean sheet." He contrasted meditation with the self-destructive methods of Vincent Van Gogh and Dylan Thomas, and of Paul Gauguin, who destroyed his family and died of syphilis halfway around the world from them.[27]

Lennon had already traveled that road. Reflecting on the lessons of his own reliance on drugs and alcohol to stimulate creativity, he compared the cost of that path with the alternative one taken by spiritual figures such as Jesus, Buddha, and Milarepa—the path involving fasting, prayer, and meditation. They and others like them had explored the territory of God for thousands of years. Wasn't it wiser to use the time-tested methods of inspiration?

7

Cynicism

Lennon benefited in yet another way from his experience with the Maharishi—in having his cynicism reinforced.

As a philosophy, Cynicism dates back twenty-four centuries to Antisthenes, a pupil of Socrates, and to a pupil of his own, Diogenes of Sinope, whose fame exceeded that of Antisthenes. The Greek root of our word *cynic* means "dog," and their fellow citizens referred to both Antisthenes and Diogenes as dogs because of their eccentric lifestyle.

Far from feeling disparaged, the two philosophers took pride in referring to themselves by the appellation. Their view was that rather than conform to the artificiality of social behavior, we should live natural lives, as animals do, and be true to ourselves. Diogenes, in particular, carried on Socrates' mission as "gadfly" to the Greeks, constantly questioning their prized culture. He owned only one set of clothes, ate whatever he could find or whatever passing friends and strangers gave him, and lived in a large earthenware tub at the edge of town.

Diogenes scorned artificial allegiances and political power. When someone wanted to know what community he came from, he replied grandly, "I am a citizen of the world." When Alexander the Great came to meet him and offered to grant him whatever he desired, Diogenes, who was sunning himself at the time, replied, "Stand out of my light."[1] He was also highly suspicious of argumentation that did not relate to the here and now. He categorized Plato's lectures about ideal forms as "a waste of time."[2]

History's most famous Cynic and John Lennon have fascinating similarities. Diogenes had a strong predisposition to speak the truth, to "say it all," no matter what the consequences. He was committed to moral freedom and contemptuous of traditional ideals. He insisted on mental independence and enjoyed defying social norms. In the words of Professor Luis E. Navia, he had "an unusual degree of intellectual lucidity, and, above all, a tremendous courage to live in accord with his convictions."[3]

Diogenes also possessed a fine sense of humor, and his displays of sarcastic wit were legendary. When Plato was commended by other thinkers for his famous definition of man as "a featherless biped," Diogenes soon showed up at the Academy. "Behold Plato's man," he declared, holding up a plucked chicken.[4] When he witnessed temple officials escorting away a man who had stolen a bowl belonging to the temple, he said, "The big thieves are leading away the little thief." When he went to a public bath that was dirty, he asked, "When people bathe here, where are they to go to get clean?" While he was asking for alms from an ill-tempered man, the man said, "I will give you, but only if you can persuade me." Diogenes responded, "If I could have persuaded you of anything, I would have persuaded you to hang yourself."[5] It's easy to imagine John Lennon delivering any of those lines—in Liverpudlian phraseology, of course.

During the two millennia between Diogenes and the present time, the disdain Cynics felt for political power and social conventions became transformed by their successors into a nihilistic attitude toward all human endeavors, beliefs, and values. In time the cynical point of view came to be characterized as simply pessimism.

In fact, however, a cynical person is not necessarily either pessimistic or optimistic. The modern definition of the term focuses narrowly on human motivations. A cynic, according to *Webster's Deluxe Unabridged Dictionary*, is "a person who believes that people are motivated in all their actions entirely by selfishness."

With the possible exception of politicians, no one gets more practice discovering the selfish motivations lurking behind veils of false sincerity than the rich and famous. Having capped his street education in Liverpool and Hamburg, with postgraduate work amid the sycophants, shysters, and parasites that could always be found swarming around the Beatles, Lennon was a cynic of world-class caliber.

He had known very well that the Maharishi's principal interest in the Beatles was to exploit their fame to help market his method of meditation to the world. But his hunger to find a mission in life allowed him to close his eyes to the fact that perfected humans exist only in religious literature and legend. His error almost surely derived from the guru's exotic persona—a strangely garbed Yogi from the Himalayas. Would he have plunged so readily into the same movement if its leader had been someone less exotic—say Reggie Dwight from Middlesex, whose favored garb was not a flowing robe but loud shirts and platform shoes?

The decade from 1966 to 1975, Lennon's long, dark night of the soul, assailed him with a string of experiences that reaffirmed his cynicism, and the years of his own personal and intellectual maturation coincided with the arrival of an era of cynicism in the Western world—particularly in the United States.

The irony of this last point is that in popular culture the period was supposed to mark the dawning of the Age of Aquarius, the astrological epoch in which war and strife and inequalities would be transcended, to be replaced by harmony and understanding among the peoples of the planet. The tsunami of post–World War II children helped fuel this myth and expectation because of their innocence and the idealism of their age-group. Their flower-power vision inevitably collided with the realities of entrenched bureaucracies, plutocracies, and ideologies, but they trusted that the barriers would crumble eventually under the weight of the un-folding cosmic plan.

The baby-boom generation did achieve some positive lasting effects in the areas of ethnic and racial sensitivity and women's liberation, but in the end, of course, even the mightiest tsunami spends its force and the continent remains. Every year more members of the generation had to find work and integrate into the "system," regardless of its flaws. Innocent people continued to die in meaningless battles, while weapons manufacturers tallied profits. Marijuana users continued to be arrested, while smokers addicted to nicotine were assigned to their juries. Rich white men gave stirring speeches about equality and then returned home in the evening to their own exclusive neighborhoods. Leaders who stood for change and compassion were cut down by assassins' bullets. In time, the post–World War II wave of young people had to conclude what every other generation ultimately has had to conclude—that no matter how ardently we might like to orient society toward grand ideals, the driving force of human interaction is self-interest.

Whether or not Lennon believed, in line with the dictionary definition, that *all* human actions are based *entirely* on selfishness, he certainly projected the image of a cynic, and his life experiences in his darkest decade gave him ample justification. Time after time the lesson was driven home to him—personally, professionally, and in the political and societal arenas as well.

When Lennon became rich and world famous as a Beatle, Alfred, the father who had not bothered to contact him in the twenty years since their traumatic separation in Blackpool, suddenly tried to reenter his life. When John ignored the exploratory letters he wrote, Freddie let it be known to a newspaper reporter that he was washing dishes for a living only a short distance from where his rich and famous son had a mansion.[6]

Because of the awkward publicity, John had no choice but to relent and meet him, and for the next few years they had an uneasy relationship in which Freddie made efforts to ingratiate himself and John dispensed money and favors. John briefly even let his father live in his Weybridge home—until he made advances toward Cynthia and John shoved him out the door. Freddie eventually married a nineteen-year-old Beatles fan and by his behavior became persona non grata. Only when he contracted cancer in the seventies and was near death did John reconcile with him again.[7]

In 1967, confronted with a tax situation in which they would owe three million pounds to Britain's Inland Revenue department unless they came up with a way to spend the money on business investment, Lennon and the other Beatles decided to start a quixotic enterprise. The company, which they named Apple, was organized into four divisions—music, merchandising, films, and electronics. They gave it the objective of demonstrating that a capitalist enterprise did not have to be a sterile, profit-driven undertaking.[8]

Lennon imagined, among other things, flamboyant New Age clothing sold by a sales staff of free-spirited "flower children," a fleet of Rolls-Royce limousines decorated in a psychedelic design like his own, discotheques based on the Sgt. Pepper theme, a motion picture division that produced innovative films, and a record label that focused on realizing its artists' visions and was free of the type of executives with whom the Beatles had to interact.

However, and partly because of the loss of the guiding hand of Brian Epstein, they had no one to shepherd the varied enterprises. Management positions were awarded to friends of the group regardless of experience. Lines of authority were blurred, operating systems never worked out, and activities left uncoordinated.

According to the publicity for the record label, for example, "The promise was that all sincere supplicants would be given encouragement, succour, a contract and maybe an envelope full of money."[9] Yet no preparations were made to process the inevitable avalanche of submissions from aspiring performers and songwriters, and most of the packages and letters wound up unopened in back rooms and the basement.

Employees worked in a party atmosphere, with liquor and drugs constantly available and expense accounts inflated by meals at the finest restaurants and extravagant business trips. Much of the clothing in the Apple boutique on Baker Street was never paid for, stolen either by shoplifters emboldened by the blasé attitude of the sales staff or by the employees themselves. Money began to flow out of the operations in a torrent—Lennon later estimated twenty thousand British pounds a week. By July 1968, the experiment collapsed, the only vestige of Apple being the recording label, which released the last few albums before the Beatles disbanded.

The process of the group's disintegration was another reaffirmation of the value of cynicism. Lennon had been haunted by an acute sense of meaninglessness ever since his arrival at the summit of society. He found no solace in religion—either traditional avenues such as Christianity or Aquarian Age alternatives such as the Maharishi's—and his marriage to

Cynthia was primarily just a result of her pregnancy with Julian. Drugs were a distraction, not a solution. His only source of orientation was his close friendships with the people he had known in Liverpool, chiefly the other three Beatles.

That safety net began to unravel. Starr and Harrison married and increasingly led independent lives. Harrison, maturing as a songwriter, resented the patronizing attitude of Lennon and McCartney about his compositions. McCartney grew ever more restless in the shadow of the outspoken Lennon—"the intellectual Beatle," the prime mover of the group. Rather than live near the other Beatles in the suburbs, he purchased a home in St. John's Wood, near the Abbey Road studios, and began cultivating relationships with the upper crust in London.

McCartney seized Brian Epstein's death as an opportunity and argued that the group no longer needed a manager—they should manage themselves; then he positioned himself to hold the reins. The others acquiesced at first to his initiative, but they grew increasingly irritated by his leadership. Personal animosities that had built up over the course of a decade began to spill out into the group's social interactions and professional life together, aggravating Lennon's sense of rootlessness and his despair at being trapped in the role of Beatle.

Into this strained atmosphere stepped Yoko Ono. Popular opinion made her the instrument of the group's destruction, when in fact she was simply a lifeline fate threw to Lennon. He had been looking for a way to exit the Beatles ever since they stopped touring in the fall of 1966.[10]

To the other Beatles, their entourage, and the reporters who had fostered and maintained the group's "Fab Four" image, Ono seemed an ice-hearted Dragon Lady. But they were interpreting her character traits through the distorting lens of their own self-interest. The bandwagon was rolling along nicely, and the last thing they wanted was for the team's strongest horse to slip free of his traces and wander away.

To Lennon, Yoko Ono was The Answer. She rescued him emotionally, excited him physically, and stimulated him intellectually. They became consumed with each other, inseparable, symbiotic. Lennon soon found himself trampling upon an unspoken code among the Beatles, that they four were "mates" and their women were auxiliaries not allowed into the inner circle. The others were distressed to learn that they could never interact with him without Yoko there at his side. He further affronted them by bringing her to the recording studio—until then a sanctuary where the four could be themselves and create their music without distractions. An artist herself, and their senior by several years, she began to offer comments about what they were doing, bruising egos.

Lennon recognized that he was shaking up the status quo, but he did not foresee how harsh the response would be to Yoko Ono. He said in a 1970 interview, "George insulted her right to her face in the Apple office at the beginning, just being straightforward, that game of, 'Well, I'm going to be up front because this is what I've heard and Dylan and a few people said you've got a lousy name in New York and you give off bad vibes.' That's what George said to her, and we both sat through it. And I didn't hit him. I don't know why. . . . Ringo was all right. So was Maureen. But the other two really gave it to us. I'll never forgive them."[11]

McCartney's disapproval came out in more subtle ways. While the Beatles were recording "Get Back" in the studio, Lennon observed that every time his writing partner sang the line "Get back to where you once belonged" he would look at Yoko. McCartney made a point of overtly consoling Cynthia Lennon after Lennon had coldly cut her out of his life. On a drive out to visit her he wrote a song, "Hey Jules," to cheer up Lennon's son Julian, which he later transformed into "Hey Jude." It became the best selling single the Beatles would ever release.[12]

The inner circle of their assistants joined in the rejection, treating Ono as though she were wallpaper. Beatles fans outside their offices and studios taunted her. The media, anxious to keep the Beatles in the lovable "Fab Four" box in which they had been packaged, also attacked her with references to her Asian features that thinly disguised racism.

Lennon could not fail to recognize how the group was splintering, but he was too much in love with Yoko to take any other course. He was also frustrated that the other Beatles, his closest friends, could not be happy for him. Worse than that, they seemed to want to punish him for finding someone he truly loved.

As the group disintegrated, everyone reacted in accordance with his own self-interest.[13] McCartney proposed that they should have professional management and lobbied for Lee Eastman, an urbane New York lawyer who just happened to be the father of the woman he was preparing to marry. Then Lennon countered by backing Allen Klein, a street-savvy, profanity-spouting man who, like Lennon, had lost his mother at a young age. As the two Beatles wrangled, trying to sway Harrison and Starr—both of whom, at different times, physically walked out on the group—word came that a third party had stabbed them both in the back.

Dick James, who held a substantial percentage of the shares of their publishing company, Northern Songs, and had been considered trustworthy for years, surreptitiously arranged to sell his shares to the British entertainment conglomerate ATV. James, witness to the mounting friction in the group, sensed the approaching breakup and simply wanted to exit while he could get the best price.[14]

Lennon made his final decision about breaking up the band in September 1969. He confided it to Allen Klein on the flight back from the Toronto Rock 'n' Roll Festival, where Lennon had found it liberating to perform an impromptu concert with Eric Clapton and Klaus Voormann instead of the other Beatles. Because business negotiations were in a delicate stage and huge advance payments had not yet been made, Klein pleaded with him to hold off disclosing his decision to anyone—even Paul McCartney. Lennon grudgingly went along with the request, but the inner turmoil proved too great and he soon called a meeting in which he told the stunned McCartney that he wanted "a divorce."[15] McCartney then, over the next six months, secretly began to work on the album that would launch his solo career, and once he was prepared to release and promote it he delivered the historic announcement of the breakup himself.

Feeling besieged by everyone from the media to his oldest and closest friends, Lennon revealed his state of mind during this period in "The Ballad of John and Yoko," a mini-autobiography in which he expressed his impression that the world was out to crucify him.

The foundations of his life were battered almost daily. His relationship with Yoko Ono was his only security, and his resolute efforts to rebuild his life around her seemed ill fated. Their flat in London was raided by police and they were charged with possession of cannabis resin. Yoko became pregnant, but there were complications and the child was lost in a highly publicized miscarriage. Public sympathy flowed instead toward Lennon's ex-wife Cynthia, who only days before had granted him a divorce.

Lennon and Ono began to take heroin to deal with the pain of the attacks and their alienation. Before long they realized the gravity of what they were doing and chose to put an end to the addiction by going cold turkey, an excruciating experience Lennon turned into a haunting song with that name. A brilliant piece of art, the song suffered commercially because it was erroneously assumed to promote the use of drugs—authorities simply refused to consider that the gut-wrenching pain it described could serve as a powerful deterrent to would-be users.

In early 1970, Lennon received in the mail a copy of a book titled *The Primal Scream*, by California psychologist Arthur Janov. Janov had developed a new therapy he claimed would cure neurotics—a therapy that involved stripping the patient of all defenses and encouraging him or her to vent repressed emotions physically, through screaming. Intrigued by the technique and the testimonials, and for that matter the title of the book itself, Lennon suggested to Yoko Ono that they contact Janov. They subsequently undertook several months of personal therapy in London and California.

For Lennon, releasing painful emotions repressed since childhood was a catharsis. He said in a 1980 *Playboy* interview, "My defenses were so great. I mean the cocky chip-on-the-shoulder, macho, aggressive rock 'n' roll hero who knew all the answers and the smart quip, the sharp-talking king of the world, was actually a terrified guy who didn't know how to cry."[16] Once again, just as in his experience with the Maharishi, he subordinated his cynicism to his hope that the therapy could benefit him. Once again a moment of disillusionment with the guru would come.

Before that moment came, however, he discovered a powerful insight about the psychological impact of not having a father during his formative years. Further, he saw its implication for society in general. Even

people who, unlike him, had fathers who did not abandon them nevertheless often suffered from a psychological void because the father was *mentally* absent—focused on interests or responsibilities outside the family.
Lennon realized that many adults, to compensate, subconsciously filled
that void in the way they gave respect to political or religious leaders.

Leaders were substitute fathers. How many people felt naturally inclined to do as their fathers told them? How many people felt comfortable
challenging their fathers?

Ultimately Lennon recognized that Arthur Janov, too, like the Maharishi before him, was just one more substitute father in his life. To assert his
independence, he would need to confront the man. The revelatory moment
came the day Janov brought in cameras to film their session. "Even under
a daddy I'm not going to be filmed," he said in a 1980 *Playboy* interview,
"especially rolling around the floor screaming. So then he started to berate
us: 'Some people are so big they won't be filmed.' He said he just happened
to be filming that session. 'Who are you kidding, Mr. Janov?' He just happened to be filming the session with John and Yoko in it."[17] However, just
as with the Maharishi, Lennon did take away something positive from the
Primal Scream experience—a new openness with his feelings. He said in
the same *Playboy* interview, "At first I was bitter about Maharishi being
human and bitter about Janov being human. Well, I'm not bitter anymore.
They're human and I'm only thinking what a dummy I was, you know.
Although I meditate and I cry."[18]

Lennon's cynicism was also reinforced by international events and the
bureaucrats, politicians, and military authorities who managed them.
During the second half of the sixties, the Vietnam War escalated into one
of the central issues of world politics. No one quite understood how it had
metamorphosed from an irritating gnat into a voracious Moloch, but by
the last two years of the decade it had polarized the consciences of average people. Bedrock America and international conservatives pushed
the domino theory and the need to defend freedom wherever it might be
threatened around the world by "godless Communism." However, the generation with no personal memory of World War II questioned an assign-
ment to fight and die in remote jungles to defend a corrupt puppet regime

against a former ally—a folk hero who had the laudable goal of liberating his homeland from foreign domination. Those who responded by fleeing to Canada and other sanctuaries to avoid the draft were disdained by the first group; those who chose to do their duty and serve in the war were reviled by the second group and sometimes spat upon when they returned from their mission.

Because of its "special relationship" with the United States and its determination to stand up against Communism around the world, the British government gave unequivocal support to the U.S. war effort. However, as the conflict escalated and the carnage grew, more British citizens began to question that policy.

As the Beatles crisscrossed America on their tours, they were often asked about the Vietnam War in interviews. For a time Brian Epstein persuaded them to avoid addressing the subject, knowing that criticism would tarnish the Beatles' lovable image and negatively impact sales. But as the antiwar movement swelled in size and Lennon kept being asked for his opinion, his conscience would no longer allow him to remain silent. Unable to play the publicity game any longer, he finally burst out with the truth. Fortunately, the eruption came at a favorable moment.

In the highly publicized interview in which he was compelled to apologize for his comments about the Beatles being more popular than Jesus, the roomful of reporters were so focused on that issue that they overlooked his response to a subsequent question about the war. He openly deplored President Johnson's recent escalation of the war by bombing Hanoi.[19]

Immediately following the end of that tour—the "Jesus Christ Tour" as the Beatles referred to it—Lennon accepted an offer to act in a film with an antiwar message. In *How I Won the War*, director Richard Lester's goal was to confront the stereotype of war movies and show the idiotic side of armed conflict: "One of the gross obscenities about war is the war film itself. War on the screen is treated like a great big adventure with extras being killed in the way of a Western."[20] Lennon played Private Gripweed, a wisecracking soldier who is led by an incompetent officer on a mission to build a cricket pitch in the German-controlled North African desert. Gripweed is ultimately killed in an insignificant skirmish.

The war in Vietnam was the prime mover in the public's shift to cynicism in the decade of the seventies. Of the 58,000 Americans who died in the war, more than 22,000 were killed following the 1969 inauguration of Richard Nixon, whose campaign promise had been a secret plan to end the conflict. Estimates of the number of Vietnamese, both North and South, who perished range from one million to two million.

In the end the reunification the United States and its allies had derailed since 1954 simply took place two decades late, and the cynics of the world noted that no one benefited from the delay except manufacturers and contractors connected with the military effort. Cynics who lived long enough were rewarded with a final bitter irony in 1995 when the United States government reestablished full diplomatic relations with the former enemy. The justification for the massive buildup of U.S. forces in Vietnam had been the nighttime attack by a North Vietnamese gunboat on a U.S. destroyer in August 1964. President Lyndon Johnson asked Congress for a resolution to give him authority to respond to the provocation, and the lawmakers complied with the Gulf of Tonkin Resolution. Decades later historians determined there had been no attack on the U.S. destroyer—only misinterpreted images on a radar screen at a time when Johnson was looking for a means to sway public opinion in favor of increased American involvement in the war.

The war polarized feelings on both sides of the Atlantic, and antiwar and antidraft protests—coupled with riots in 125 American cities following the April 4, 1968, assassination of Dr. Martin Luther King, Jr., (which took 55,000 federal and national guard troops to suppress)[21] and frequent demonstrations in favor of women's liberation and reproductive rights—created a climate in which some began to call for a complete renovation of the system. The summer of 1967 had been labeled "the Summer of Love." Just a year later, the most passionate of the protestors were calling for a violent revolution.

Lennon, tempering idealism with cynicism, never lost his hope for an egalitarian, loving, and peaceful society, but he was dubious about the motivations and shortsightedness of those who seemed to advocate destroying the world in order to save it. Any cynical observer could see that the powerful elite of the Western countries were more committed to perpetuating their control and maintaining their perquisites than to pursuing such ideals as justice and equality, but would overthrowing them and their system in a bloody revolution achieve the positive end desired?

As a perceived leader of the rebellious Left, Lennon was looked to for inspiration. In August 1968, he responded with a song directed to the people who regarded him as a guiding light. In "Revolution," he agreed with their belief that the world needed changing, but to those who advocated using violent methods he sent out a simple message: if the method of change they proposed involved destruction, he wanted no part of it. Disputing their belief that the problem was with "the institution," he countered that they ought to concentrate instead on freeing their own minds.

For Lennon, a successful revolution required a change in society's state of mind. Violent action would result only in destruction, but an elevation of consciousness would make change irresistible. Less than a year after the release of the song, he and Yoko would attempt to further that aim through a performance-based, event-oriented media campaign.

A few weeks before his death, in a major interview with *Playboy* magazine, he commented about "Revolution": "The lyrics stand today. They're still my feeling about politics. . . . Count me out if it's for violence. Don't expect me on the barricades unless it is with flowers. As far as overthrowing something in the name of Marxism or Christianity, I want to know what you're going to do *after* you've knocked it all down. I mean, can't we use *some* of it? What's the point of bombing Wall Street? If you want to change the system, change the system. It's no good shooting people."[22]

In spite of Lennon's own rebellious nature and his personal despair, and in spite of the fact that he sympathized with the demagogues' point of view and their frustration, he could not accept the simple solutions they promoted with their own agendas.

Lennon had reached his intellectual maturity rejecting, or at least questioning, the beliefs and social norms his culture had handed him, while opening his mind to new possibilities and paradigms. As a freethinker he felt comfortable experimenting with new perspectives, indulging whims, even getting passionate about alternative lifestyles and worldviews. But he never lost his jeweler's-eye cynicism. He could coldly and abruptly abandon any pathway proved illusory or any that was misrepresented by someone with less than honorable motives. In the end he clung to his independence, no matter what the cost to his psyche, struggling to find his own way.

Lennon's long, dark night would extend halfway through the decade of the seventies—through his flirtation with the New Left, his harassment at the hands of the FBI and the INS, and the "lost weekend" in which he threw himself headlong into a mire of alcohol and drugs. Even so, the bedrock he was always desperate to find first appeared in the last months of the sixties. It came as a result of his union with Yoko Ono, who served, in their multifaceted relationship, as his liberator, pole star, and prod. Rescued by her, he gradually managed to emerge from the glass exhibition case in which the public had attempted to label him and lock him away—as the "mop-top" rock superstar—and to rediscover himself as the more broadly defined capital-A "Artist."

Years would pass, but the painful reinvention that began in mid-1968 based on his relationship with Yoko Ono made it possible for him to achieve his greatest work, a work created on the canvas of life.

Suggested Listening
"A Day in the Life"
"All You Need Is Love"
"Revolution"
"God"
"I Found Out"

PART THREE

LIFE AS A WORK OF ART

8

Reborn Artist

John Lennon's first encounter with Yoko Ono came, fittingly, at an art gallery. One November evening in 1966, he accepted the invitation of John Dunbar, owner of the Indica Gallery in London, to attend the opening of a new exhibit.

After the Beatles had stopped touring in August, Lennon, out of fear of being idle, immediately plunged into the filming of *How I Won the War*. Once that ended and he returned to London, he began to make the rounds of the city's art galleries for the same reason—as well as to acquaint himself with the current trends in art. Now Dunbar had piqued his curiosity with a comment that he was hosting a major new talent from the United States—a female Japanese avant-garde artist—and that there would be a mysterious "happening" involving climbing into a black bag with someone. Lennon found the prospect titillating because there was an insinuation of removing clothing and having sex.

When he arrived, however, Lennon discovered that he had come a day early; the show was still being installed. Touring the premises, he noted a pair of bent nails on a plastic box. Next he saw a fresh apple placed on a stand labeled simply "Apple." Lennon recalled what happened next in *Playboy* shortly before his death in 1980. John Dunbar came along with Yoko Ono in tow to meet the millionaire Beatle, and she handed him a card. On it was a single word: "Breathe." "And I said, 'You mean [*panting*]?' She says, 'That's it. You've got it.' And I'm thinking, I've got it! [*Laughs*] But I'm all geared up to *do* something. I want to do something."

Lennon noticed a ladder whose steps led up to a painting on the ceiling, which was accompanied by a dangling magnifying glass.

It's what made me stay. I went up the ladder and I got the spyglass and there was tiny little writing there. . . . You're on this ladder—you feel like a fool—you could fall any minute—and you look through and it just says "YES."

Well, all the so-called avant-garde art at the time and everything that was supposedly interesting was all negative, this smash-the-piano-with-a-hammer, break-the-sculpture boring, negative crap. It was all anti-, anti-, anti-. Anti-art, anti-establishment. And just that "YES" made me stay in a gallery full of apples and nails instead of just walking out. . . .

Then I went up to this thing that said, "Hammer a nail in." I said, "Can I hammer a nail in?"

Ono demurred, wanting to keep the exhibit pristine for the next day's opening. John Dunbar—knowing that it was not wise to refuse a patron so wealthy he could buy the whole show on a whim—began trying to persuade her to allow it.

Lennon was amused: "So there was this little conference and she finally said, 'OK, you can hammer a nail in for five shillings.' So smart-ass here says, 'Well, I'll give you an imaginary five shillings and hammer an imaginary nail in.' And that's when we really *met*. That's when we locked eyes and she got it and I got it and that was it. The rest, as they say in all the interviews we do, is history."[1]

Ono kept in contact with Lennon. She had published a book of instructional poems two years earlier, titled *Grapefruit*. She sent him a copy at the Abbey Road studio where the Beatles recorded their music. When he visited the London headquarters of the Spiritual Regeneration Movement to join and receive his mantra, she also went, specifically to meet him again.[2]

Fascinated by her, Lennon underwrote her Half-A-Wind show, which ran from mid-October to mid-November of 1967 in the Lisson Gallery. In keeping with the theme, visitors to the gallery were confronted with a variety of items—a bed and pillow, a washbasin, a toothbrush—each cut neatly in half. Lennon appreciated Ono's offbeat sense of humor and thought-provoking art, but he kept his patronage anonymous. The show was credited "Yoko Plus Me."[3]

Ono's book of poems stayed by Lennon's bedside in Kenwood, and during the months he was away in India with the Maharishi she regularly sent him letters and postcards with mystifying, poetic messages: "I'm a cloud. Watch for me in the sky."[4]

Over time her eccentric, art-oriented personality aroused in him the spirit that had been nearly asphyxiated under layers of pop music success ever since his days at the Liverpool College of Art. Not since his long conversations with Stu Sutcliffe had he found someone whose ideas on art so stimulated and challenged him.

Lennon convinced himself when he departed for India that in the Maharishi's movement he had at last discovered the direction he was supposed to go. Life in the ashram cleansed his system of drugs and alcohol, filled his lungs with fresh air, restored him physically with wholesome vegetarian meals, and recharged him mentally through hours of daily meditation. But he experienced no brain-altering flash of enlightenment under the bo tree, and as the weeks passed his mind began to wander. No longer subject to the frantic pace of a Beatle, he had time to reflect. He had the unexpected liberty to reconsider his life, his relationships, and his art—to ponder where he had ended up and muse about where he really wanted to be.

In the midst of a retreat focused on serenity and spiritual regeneration, and in the daily company of his wife, Cynthia, he wrote "Yer Blues," whose lyrics revealed an alienated state of mind and even openly expressed thoughts of suicide.

When he returned to England—no longer restrained by his pledge to the Maharishi to avoid drugs and alcohol—and found himself spiraling downward into dissipation and despair, his thoughts gravitated toward the mysterious Japanese artist who wanted to be with him. Cynthia and Julian took a trip to Greece in the company of Alex Mardas and Jenny Boyd, the sister of George Harrison's wife, Pattie. While she was gone, Lennon invited Yoko Ono to come out to his Weybridge home late one May night. He took her up to his home recording studio, filled with a network of tape recorders and other equipment, and played her an experimental aural collage he was working on, which would later appear on the Beatles' *White Album* under the title "Revolution 9." Then, to occupy themselves, they began improvising. They spent all night working on a piece that would one day be released as their joint creation, *Two Virgins*. Then, at dawn, they made love.[5]

His friend Pete Shotton was also staying in the house that night. When Shotton came down to breakfast, Lennon asked if he would mind going out to find a new house to purchase. Shotton asked why, and Lennon shocked him by saying that he had decided to move into a new house with Yoko Ono. "This is *it*, Pete. This is what I've been waiting for all me life."[6]

Lennon's life did change, abruptly and irrevocably. For him it was a rebirth. From the viewpoint of the outside world his situation might have been enviable, but in his heart he felt he had lost control of his own destiny. The unprecedented success of the Beatles had swallowed him up, and he was being hustled forward down a narrow corridor by the obligations of recording contracts and the expectations of fans and the media. He had nowhere to turn for help; the coterie of aides and hangers-on who surrounded him had a stake in his persona as Beatle John and facilitated his captivity. "The king is always killed by his courtiers, not by his enemies. The king is overfed, overdrugged, overindulged, anything to keep the king tied to his throne. Most people in that position never wake up. They either die mentally or physically or both. And what Yoko did for me, apart from liberating me to be a feminist, was to liberate me from that situation."[7]

The mental liberation Lennon experienced was exhilarating, and that summer and fall of 1968 he threw off his shackles with complete disregard for the opinions of anyone. Doing so was consistent with his own decisiveness, consistent with his blunt working-class personality, consistent with the untrammeled social power the Beatles possessed, and consistent with his disdain for the bourgeois conventions that had ensnared him in a fate not of his own choosing. But he would pay a fearsome price.

When Cynthia Lennon returned from Greece she discovered that her life had changed, too, abruptly and irrevocably. She took solace in wine and a night with Lennon's friend Alex Mardas. She and John tried for a while to maintain a fiction that nothing had changed, but when she took a preplanned trip to Italy, she received word that John was planning to divorce her. When she arrived back in London she was served with legal papers—Lennon was charging *her* with adultery over the incident with Alex Mardas.[8]

Lennon had now openly cast his fate to the wind. He quickly began to pay the price for his freedom. The new couple might have attempted to remain out of the public eye until divorce arrangements had been made—for Ono as well as for Lennon; she was also married—but neither was temperamentally inclined to avoid controversy. Lennon, especially, favored being frank and open, no matter what the cost. Moreover, with Ono's encouragement, he felt emboldened to reassert himself as an artist.

Together, they saw an opportunity to make a statement in the National Sculpture Exhibition, which would present a selection of the best contemporary British sculpture. John came up with the concept of planting a pair of acorns in the ground, one facing east, the other west, symbolic of their own love as well as the uniting and growth of two cultures.[9]

While the controlling committee was willing to accept their entry because of Lennon's stature as a celebrity and the publicity it would guarantee, they declined to acknowledge the work in the exhibition's official catalog. Lennon and Ono responded by simply publishing their own document. In it John's statement read, "This is what happens when two clouds meet." Opposite that was Yoko's statement: "This is what happens when two clouds meet (the piece is John's idea but it was so good that I stole it)."[10]

A harsher rebuff awaited them. The main sculptures in the exhibition were to be placed around the grounds of Coventry Cathedral. When Lennon and Ono arrived on the day of the preview with their acorns, they were met by the religious official in charge, Canon Verney, who informed them that because of their status as an unwed couple, both with other spouses, he could not allow them to plant the acorns on consecrated ground. After some tense exchanges, made worse by Verney's pronouncement that the acorns weren't really sculpture anyway, the parties reached a compromise.

The artists were allowed to plant the acorns on the grounds surrounding the cathedral—unconsecrated ground.[11]

Two weeks later, on July 1, 1968, Lennon gave his first art exhibition, which took place at the prestigious Robert Frazer Gallery on Duke Street. He used the occasion to announce publicly his relationship with Ono, dedicating it "To Yoko from John. With Love."

Lennon's eccentric wit drove the event. The centerpiece was a huge white circular canvas on which he had written the show's title, You Are Here—a lighthearted recognition of the patron's visit, but beyond that a surreally funny phrase to London residents, who associated it with locating their positions on subway maps. To approach the canvas the visitor had first to wind through a series of collection boxes soliciting funds for a variety of whimsical charities, from The National Canine Defense League to The Sons of the Divine Providence. Lennon even continued the exhibition outside, releasing 365 white balloons to the four winds, each carrying a note asking for a response from the finder of the grounded balloon.[12]

Given the show's levity, Lennon was unprepared for the acrimony it provoked. One critic called it "not even Pop Art, it's Lollypop Art." When hundreds of responses came back to the balloon invitations, few reflected the spirit with which he had launched them. Most upbraided him for his out-of-wedlock relationship, his dreadful treatment of Cynthia, his hair, his wealth, and his travesty of the world of art. He attempted to take the criticism in stride: "The trouble, I suppose, is that I've spoiled my image. People want me to stay in their own bag. They want me to be lovable. But I was never that. Even at school I was just 'Lennon.' Nobody ever thought of me as cuddly!"[13]

The public had fallen in love with the witty rapscallion from *A Hard Day's Night*. They had been willing to broaden their view of him when he led the call for "flower power" and had his Rolls-Royce repainted in a paisley design. Many had even grudgingly accepted his infatuation with the strange little Yogi from India as just the eccentric behavior of a man whose lofty goal was to bring love to the world. But now he seemed completely out of his mind, involved in a headlong plunge to outrage society and to alienate his supporters.

In a few short months he squandered years of accrued good will. On August 22, as a result of his openly flaunted relationship with Yoko Ono, Cynthia countersued him for divorce.[14] On October 18, police raided the flat where he and Ono were living, discovering 219 grains of cannabis resin—even though Lennon had been previously tipped off about the raid and had thoroughly cleaned the premises. (Four years later the arresting officer was sentenced to two years in prison for planting evidence in another case.)[15] On October 25, while still officially married to Cynthia, Lennon announced that he and Yoko were expecting a baby in February 1969. On November 8, Cynthia was granted a divorce in court. On November 21, Yoko had a miscarriage of the out-of-wedlock child while in bed at Queen Charlotte's Maternity Hospital. On November 28, Lennon accepted lone responsibility for the unauthorized possession of cannabis resin, and after pleading guilty was fined 150 pounds plus twenty guineas.

The very next day, in an act that showed stunning disregard for public opinion, Lennon and Ono released *Unfinished Music No. 1: Two Virgins*, an avant-garde album composed of the recordings they had made together on their all-night session in May. However, what made the album so controversial was not the content but the cover photograph, which showed them both in full frontal nudity.

Many people who heard the news (few saw the cover) concluded that Lennon definitely had gone crazy. He responded to the uproar: "The picture was to prove that we are not a couple of demented freaks and that we are not deformed in any way and that our minds are healthy. If you think that it was obscene, it can only have been so in your own mind. For us it was the culmination of our love for one another and of how we thought that love might be useful to others."[16]

From the point of view of the average member of a Western society in 1968 (and even today), Lennon *had* gone crazy. What mature, "normal" person would disseminate his nude photograph to the public at large? Who would print it on a commercial product and expect record shops to display the album cover in their racks alongside those of Petula Clark and Herman's Hermits? Who would justify his action by asserting he was trying to prove that his mind was healthy?

Lennon, however, was not crazy. He was correct that the obscenity was in the viewer's mind. And he was correct that his mind was healthy.

Assume for a moment that aliens from an advanced civilization arrive on Earth to observe us the way our anthropologists observe primitive cultures in remote areas. They dutifully record in their notebooks that we are bipedal creatures with sparse hair on our bodies who long ago learned to cover our skin to keep warm during periods when our surroundings are uncomfortably cold. Over time we developed some very curious customs regarding those outer coverings.

For example, we find it discourteous and sometimes even illegal for male bipeds to walk around in public places without a covering on the upper half of their bodies—except, that is, when they are beside the sea or a lake, or in the proximity of small artificial bodies of water surrounded by webbed chairs. For female bipeds this prohibition is even more rigorously enforced, excused only on the southern coast of France or in a strange and irredeemable city called Las Vegas—in spite of the fact that numerous cultures from around the planet once regarded the behavior as commonly accepted practice.

Neither gender has the right to walk around without protective fabric covering the lower half of the body, except in certain areas clearly designated as "nudist camps." These prohibitions apply even though the vast majority of adult bipeds see naked members of the opposite sex every day inside their dwellings and even though crowds of bipeds regularly view naked representatives of their species on huge white screens.

Cultural norms are simply that—cultural norms. When looked at from a completely objective point of view, they seem like strange behavior. Just how would aliens view our eccentricities? Pause for a moment and visualize going to a zoo. There you see two gorillas dressed in suits and ties, both appalled by the sight of a third gorilla strolling around naked.

What inclined Lennon to show himself unclothed was not insanity but an uncommon commitment to honesty. Finding a kindred spirit in Yoko Ono released him from the mental shackles of "normalcy." Alone, he was an aberration—a married, suburban-dwelling father who, although highly creative and successful, always secretly worried that his radically iconoclastic worldview might mean he was crazy. Discovering and falling in love with a woman who was capable of seeing things as he did, he felt vindicated, supported, liberated, reborn. Weary with observing social artifices and conventions for the sake of appearances, he wanted to live honestly. *Completely* honestly.

Lennon at first had planned to release the record as Ono's alone, and he thought she should be nude on the cover "because her work is naked, basically simple and childlike and truthful."[17] Then it dawned on him that the work could represent a statement by both of them to the world: Here we are, deeply in love, newly born, virginal, completely unpretentious, and honest with both ourselves and with you the audience.

That his decision to expose himself naked to the public eye was an artistic statement and not some display of perverted exhibitionism was confirmed by an incident that took place years later. Lennon and Ono had invited their friend and confidant Elliot Mintz to visit their rented home near Santa Barbara, California. It being a hot summer day, the three went outside to the swimming pool. While Mintz was enjoying the sight of Ono lying on the diving board, he heard movement behind him. He turned to find Lennon rustling a bathrobe around himself, using it as a screen in order discreetly to pull off his trousers and then slip on his swimsuit. Lennon acknowledged his inquisitive glance with a smile: "I'm English, you know."[18]

The provocative cover of *Two Virgins* was the first bold step onto a pathway Lennon and Ono intended to be honest, positive, and influential, and they didn't care if it stirred up controversy. Intent on stretching artistic boundaries, they undertook a number of avant-garde projects over the next couple of years.

As a follow-up to *Two Virgins*, they released two other vinyl albums, *Unfinished Music No. 2: Life with the Lions* and *The Wedding Album*. The first included Ono's improvised vocalizations at a concert in Cambridge, accompanied by Lennon playing guitar feedback. Another sequence featured the tape-recorded heartbeat of the child she had miscarried. The second album dedicated an entire side to the two calling out each other's names in a spectrum of emotional tones against the percussion of their recorded heartbeats, with the second side devoted to an aural collage from their first bed-in event for peace.

The two also produced a string of experimental films, beginning with *Smile* in August 1968, in which Lennon's smile came to life in super slow motion over the course of a fifty-minute film. *Fly, Rape, Up Your Legs Forever, Self-Portrait, Apotheosis,* and *Erection* followed, among others. Ono's *Fly,* for example, follows in extreme close-ups the progress of a housefly making its way along the apparent mountains, valleys, and plains of a naked female body. Lennon's *Erection* offers a time-lapse view of the building of a massive new hotel. Months of construction are compressed into just minutes of film.[19]

Lennon also produced work in a more traditional medium, though he still managed to generate controversy. Bag One, the Erotic Lithographs, debuted in the London Arts Gallery in January 1970. The collection consisted of three hundred sets of fourteen prints, each executed in the black-line drawing style for which he was noted. The subject matter covered his wedding and honeymoon with Ono, including some very explicit drawings of the two of them unclothed.

Scotland Yard raided the gallery on the second day, confiscating eight of the lithographs deemed to be "indecent." Months later, when the case at last came to court, the defense presented a number of Picasso drawings for comparison and the magistrate in charge ultimately declared that the prints were "unlikely to deprave or corrupt."[20]

All of these works, however, were far overshadowed by a project Lennon and Ono jointly created using the medium of real life. The inspiration for this most ambitious undertaking was a letter sent to them by Peter Watkins, producer of the film *The War Game.*[21] The British Broadcasting Corporation had commissioned the film to educate the public about the grim reality behind the hazy concept of nuclear war. What Watkins brought back to them was a film so intense, horrifying, and politically incendiary that the BBC management decided it could not be aired. In his letter to Lennon and Ono, Watkins decried the control of the media and stated that people in their position—with such easy access to it—bore a responsibility to use their open door for the benefit of world peace. He closed his letter with the challenge, "What are you going to do about it?"

Deeply affected, they considered for three weeks how they could respond to the challenge before finally coming up with a brilliant and unprecedented event, centered on their upcoming wedding. The event not only made international headlines, it transformed their approach to the world. They were two gifted artists, and they determined to use the resources at their disposal to create something new—their life itself would become the artwork.

9

PEACE ADVOCATE

T he world's media had never seen a peace demonstration to compare with the one that awaited them in the Amsterdam Hilton in late March 1969. Witnesses to the most turbulent years of the sixties, hardened journalists had come to expect swarms of people carrying signs, blocking traffic, chanting slogans, sometimes gaining passion from their own numbers and challenging authorities, throwing rocks, and provoking fights that frequently escalated into riots. Instead, in Suite 902, the Presidential Suite, John Lennon and Yoko Ono sat in a king-size bed in their white nightwear and responded to questions, gently making the case for peace.

They characterized the event as a bed-in—the latest in a line of spin-offs from the sit-ins of the early sixties (demonstrations demanding racial equality in the American South), which had led to lie-ins, love-ins, and be-ins, among other incarnations. The provocative label guaranteed the attention of the media, since the event immediately followed the couple's marriage (on March 20, six weeks after Ono divorced her husband) and marked the beginning of their honeymoon. With the nude album cover still fresh in everyone's memory, Lennon and Ono were considered capable of *anything*.

The chief of Amsterdam's vice squad contributed to the air of salacious expectation: "If people are invited to such a 'happening,' the police would certainly act."

An announcement went out: for the seven days of their honeymoon the newlyweds would permit members of the media to come into their room from ten in the morning until eight in the evening. When ten o'clock arrived on the first day, a crowd of fifty newspeople gathered outside the door, jostling for position. "These guys were sweating to fight to get in first because they thought we were going to be making love in bed," Lennon said later, amused.[1]

When the first reporters were ushered inside, they instead discovered they were being used in a brilliant public-relations ploy. They were there to get a story, but the story turned out not to be a voyeuristic look at two crazies in heat but a radically different approach to the promotion of world peace. Lennon said in a *Playboy* interview, "When we got married, we knew our honeymoon was going to be public anyway, so we decided to use it to make a statement. Our life is our art. That's what the bed-in was. We sat in bed and talked to reporters for seven days. It was hilarious. In effect, we were doing a commercial for peace instead of a commercial for war. The reporters were going 'uh-huh, yeah, sure,' but it didn't matter because our commercial went out irrespective. As I've said, everybody puts down TV commercials, but they go around singing them."[2]

Amid a setting of flowers, drawings, and hand-painted signs with slogans and catchwords such as "Hair Peace," "Bed Peace," "I love John," and "I love Yoko," the skeptical reporters dutifully copied down the message Lennon and Ono wanted to disseminate. The revelation they preached was the possibility of alternatives to violent action—as Lennon characterized them, "in the tradition of Gandhi, only with a sense of humor." He summarized: "Protest for peace in any way, but peacefully, 'cause we think that peace is only got by peaceful methods, and that to fight the establishment with their own weapons is no good because they always win, and they've been winning for thousands of years. They know how to play the game of violence. But they don't know how to handle humor, and peaceful humor—and that's our message really."[3]

The two were perfectly content to play the fools if it advanced the cause. "The Blue Meanies, or whoever they are, are promoting violence all the time in every newspaper, every TV show and every magazine. The least

Yoko and I can do is hog the headlines and make people laugh. I'd sooner see our faces in a bed in the paper than yet another politician smiling at the people and shaking hands."[4]

Most of the media did consider the couple's actions ludicrous. Over thirty-five thousand American soldiers—and many times that number of Vietnamese—had already died in a war that most people now realized was a stalemate. The British government was sending arms to the Nigerian government to be used in its brutal suppression of Biafra, a region where hundreds of thousands of people were dying of starvation. The streets of Washington, London, and Paris were regularly clogged with tens of thousands of angry protestors. The world outside was on fire, and here John and Yoko sat in bed in a posh hotel and seemed to believe that their "protest" would help bring about world peace.

Most journalists also misjudged the sincerity of Lennon's commitment, which could easily be dismissed as the passing fancy of a self-indulgent and publicity-hungry rock star. In truth, he was deeply motivated and utterly devoted to the task. Here was another excellent opportunity, according to the insight of Viktor E. Frankl, to give life meaning by using his unique influence to try to accomplish a great goal.

Over the next few years Lennon worked zealously toward that aim. His quest for peace resonated with a passage from *The Passover Plot*. Hugh Schonfield, while making his argument against the divinity of Jesus, expressed secular admiration for the man's greatness as a human being, citing his iron commitment to the improvement of humankind through audacious action: "Because Jesus is not worshipped he is not thereby inevitably played down or diminished in effectiveness. Rather should we be strengthened and encouraged because he is bone of our bone and flesh of our flesh and no God incarnate. The mind that was in the Messiah can therefore also be in us, stimulating us to accomplish what those of more careful and nicely balanced disposition declare to be impossible. Thus the victory for which Jesus relentlessly schemed and strove will be won at last. There will be peace throughout the earth."[5]

Lennon was certainly stimulated to try to accomplish what the average person considered impossible. When skeptics dismissed his audacity as naiveté, he smiled with them and kept on striving—perfectly willing to be considered foolish if it advanced the cause—as though he saw a possibility they did not see.

As a pacifist, Lennon rejected violence as a means to achieve peace, modeling his approach on the nonviolent methods devised by Mahatma Gandhi and Dr. Martin Luther King, Jr. But their path involved mobilizing crowds of people to take part in public acts of civil disobedience designed to achieve specific objectives. Lennon wanted to try something new. He had grown up in the age of mass media and saw other, possibly more effective ways to transform social and political systems than confrontations in the streets—such as raising the level of consciousness through modern techniques. "Henry Ford knew how to sell cars by advertising. I'm selling peace, and Yoko and I are just one big advertising campaign. It may make people laugh but it may make them think, too. Really, we're Mr. and Mrs. Peace."[6]

He amplified the concept in another conversation: "The struggle is in the mind. We must bury our own monsters and stop condemning people. We are all Christ and we are all Hitler. We want Christ to win. We're trying to make Christ's message contemporary. What would he have done if he had advertisements, records, films, TV and newspapers? Christ made miracles to tell his message. Well, the miracle today is communications, so let's use it."[7]

Over the next year he experimented with various ways. When the newlyweds returned to England, they tried a more audacious and more highly publicized version of Lennon's "Two Acorn" idea for the previous summer's National Sculpture Exhibition. They sent every head of state in the world a pair of acorns to plant in every country, a symbolic suggestion that peace had to start somewhere and that perhaps acting in concert in such a simple action would stimulate the growth of peace in other ways. What they were doing in essence was the highly imaginative integration of art into politics. The world's power structures, however, failed to appreciate the artistry and symbolism behind what appeared to be a frivolous bid for publicity. Only Golda Meir of Israel and Pierre Trudeau of Canada were willing to follow through on the request.[8]

Two months after their Amsterdam bed-in, the couple recreated the event in Montreal. Lennon was barred from entering the United States because of his drug conviction the previous year, so they launched a "Radio Free America" service from just across the border in Canada. They promoted peace through a nonstop barrage of telephone interviews with U.S. radio stations and in-person meetings with the journalists and leaders of culture who came north to meet them.

Lennon's most dramatic moment came when placed on the line to students at the University of California, Berkeley, who were demonstrating in support of expropriation of an unused lot belonging to the university so that it could be turned into a People's Park. Hundreds of police had been called in, and the students, on the verge of being assaulted, excitedly asked for Lennon's advice.

His reply was probably not what they hoped to hear. "I don't believe there's any park worth getting shot for," he told them. He advised them to relocate their demonstration to another city or even go to Canada, leaving the authorities "nothing to attack and nobody to point the finger at."[9] The students failed to heed him. The assault came and over one hundred demonstrators were injured, with one left dead and one blinded.

Later during the demonstration, Lennon said, "The students are being conned! It's like the school bully: he aggravates you and aggravates you until you hit him. And then they kill you, like in Berkeley. . . . But the students have gotten conned into thinking they can change it with violence and they can't, you know, they can only make it uglier and worse."[10]

Lennon worked indefatigably to get his message across in Montreal, fielding questions from a wide range of perspectives and levels of understanding of what he and Ono were trying to achieve—confronting a torrent of skepticism with a torrent of words. In one typical exchange, an exasperated reporter who just could not grasp the relevance of their bed-bound approach asked, "What *are* you doing?" Lennon shot back an explanation just as elementary and concise as he could make it: "All we are saying is give peace a chance."[11]

Suddenly inspired, he proceeded immediately to work out the lyrics and melody to a new song so that he could record it in the same room where it had been conceived. Using a portable eight-track recorder brought in for the purpose, he solicited the backing of a chorus composed of the entourage around him—a group that included, besides Yoko Ono, Tommy Smothers, Allen Ginsberg, Dick Gregory, Petula Clark, Timothy Leary and his wife Rosemary, and the Canadian chapter of the Radha Krishna Temple.[12]

Employing humorous wordplay reminiscent of *The Daily Howl* and *In His Own Write*—Ragism? Tagism? Sinisters? Fishops?—Lennon distilled his position down to its essence. No matter what "ism" you identify with, no matter what authority you find credible, no matter what issue you consider most important, how can you dispute that peace is desirable and ought to be given a chance to work?

While trying to beguile the media with "gimmicks and salesmanship," Lennon came up with an ageless work of art. He later admitted that he had been harboring a desire to write a new song for the peace movement—something with the spirit and universality of "We Shall Overcome"—and now, at precisely the right moment, the concept, melody, and lyrics had come to him. Just as "All You Need Is Love" became the anthem for the "Love Generation," "Give Peace a Chance" became the anthem for those in the streets protesting for peace. Over two million copies of the single were purchased, and that autumn an antiwar crowd estimated at almost half a million, gathered within earshot of the White House, used it to serenade Richard Nixon.[13]

A new version of "Give Peace a Chance" was released in 1991 as the Gulf War was about to begin, performed by an ad hoc group of dozens of luminaries in the music world calling themselves the Peace Choir. Over 300,000 copies of the remake were sold, but its influence could better be measured by the reaction of the BBC. The defender of British sensibilities banned airplay for a two-decades-old song whose chorus practically every adult in the developed world knew by heart.[14]

Following the Montreal bed-in, Lennon and Ono began a program of almost constant engagement with the media about the peace message. Back in London, from their office at the headquarters of Apple, they scheduled interviews in thirty-minute blocks—often as many as fifteen in a day.

The message varied little. People needed to be made aware that the power to change things rested in their own hands. The people themselves had to seize the initiative, especially if the government would not. But they must do so without violence, which was counterproductive.

Lennon compared the steady drumbeat of the media blitz to the propaganda used by others intent on shaping public opinion. "The government can do it with propaganda. Coca-Cola can do it with propaganda. The businessmen can do it with propaganda. Why can't we? We are the hip generation."[15]

The creative media-oriented approach Lennon and Ono pursued required a stream of events to publicize. One of the most controversial came in late November. Ever since Lennon had received his title of Member of the British Empire in 1965, he felt awkward about possessing the award. Such a public pat on the head from the establishment compromised his identity as a rebel, a freethinker, an iconoclast. When he had first received notice of the upcoming honor in a letter from Queen Elizabeth's aide, he even refused to answer it, tossing it into a pile of fan mail. Brian Epstein finally learned of the nomination and sent a letter of acceptance in Lennon's name.[16]

Because the medal meant so little to him, Lennon gave it to his Aunt Mimi to keep. On November 26, 1969, he sent his chauffeur to her house in Bournemouth to retrieve it. Later that same day, Lennon and Ono dropped off the medal at Buckingham Palace. Significantly, he did so at the tradesmen's entrance, a comment on Lennon's working-class background and self-identification.[17] "I always squirmed when I saw MBE on my letters. I didn't really belong to that sort of world. I think the Establishment bought the Beatles with it. Now I am giving it back, thank you very much. Investitures are a waste of time. It's mostly hypocritical snobbery and part of the class system. I only took it to help the Beatles make the big time. I know I sold my soul when I received it, but now I have helped to redeem it in the cause of peace."[18]

Accompanying the medal when he returned it was a brief note on the stationery of Lennon and Ono's company, Bag Productions:

Your Majesty,

I am returning this MBE in protest against Britain's involvement in the Nigeria-Biafra thing, against our support of America in Vietnam, and against "Cold Turkey" slipping down the charts.

With Love,

John Lennon of Bag[19]

The announcement of the medal's return provoked a storm of indignation, in general because of the perceived snub of the queen, in particular because of the flippant reference to "Cold Turkey," which Lennon had thrown in to lighten the tone but which appeared insolent and crudely commercial.

However, the move did achieve its purpose of attracting attention to the peace movement. Philosopher Bertrand Russell, for one, wrote Lennon to praise him for publicly condemning Britain's role in the wars of Biafra and Vietnam: "Whatever abuse you have suffered in the press as a result of this, I am confident that your remarks will have caused a very large number of people to think again about these wars."[20]

On December 16, Lennon and Ono rolled out yet another inventive and high-profile media event. To hammer home once again the fact that the people have the power to direct events, if they only will seize the initiative, they came up with a simple message printed in large type.

The message? "WAR IS OVER!" In much smaller type below it were the words: "If you want it." Following that was their greeting: "Happy Christmas, John and Yoko."

To disseminate the message, they paid for its placement on billboards in prominent locations in major cities around the world—Paris, Rome, Berlin, Tokyo, Athens, Los Angeles, and New York, among others—and distributed thousands of posters in the suburbs.[21]

At the very end of the year, the final days of the turbulent sixties, they succeeded for the first time in bringing their quest for peace to the top level of government. They revisited Canada for the purpose of announcing and promoting a music festival devoted to the cause of peace—one so gigantic that it would dwarf Woodstock. While there they worked out final arrangements to meet with the leader of Canada, Prime Minister Pierre Elliott Trudeau.

Because of Lennon's public persona, a convicted drug user with a scandalous private life, given to unpredictable and outrageous behavior, no image-conscious political leader could take the gamble of a public meeting with him, even in the cause of world peace. Pierre Trudeau, however, was a maverick himself, indulging in free-spirited behavior such as public pirouettes and sitting in with jazz bands, although keeping his displays within the bounds of good taste. His image was that of an unusually broad-minded politician, always open to new ideas. For him, a meeting with Beatle John Lennon discussing the topic of world peace would add luster to that image and, of course, pay dividends in the form of support among younger voters. He agreed to meet with Lennon and Ono, his sole proviso being that no advance notice be given to the public or the media.

Two days before Christmas, the couple was ushered into Trudeau's office in the parliament buildings in Ottawa. They were allotted fifteen minutes but ultimately spent more than fifty as the conversation ranged over Lennon's poetry and books, music, the generation gap, and the ongoing peace campaign. When Lennon described the concept of the Peace Festival to be held outside Toronto, Trudeau responded favorably and even offered his government's endorsement and support.

In a press conference after the meeting, Lennon was both complimentary and politic: "If there were more leaders like Mr. Trudeau, the world would have peace. . . . You don't know how lucky you are in Canada."[22]

While the goal of the peace campaign proved elusive, Lennon's creative, heartfelt, and indefatigable efforts to use his fame and influence to strive for world peace would forever associate him with the dream in the public imagination. Along with Mahatma Gandhi and Martin Luther King, Jr., John Lennon stands out prominently as one of the twentieth century's three icons of peace.

All three would die by gunfire.

10

Social Activist

The work of art John Lennon began to create with his new life in tandem with Yoko Ono extended beyond advocacy of peace. He became an activist in a number of issues of social justice.

In November 1969, the parents of James Hanratty, a convicted murderer executed by the government, visited a wealthy nephew of theirs in Ascot. John and Yoko happened to be the nephew's neighbors. When they were introduced to Hanratty's parents and learned firsthand the details of an apparent miscarriage of justice, they were appalled and joined the calls for a public inquiry.

The crimes Hanratty had been convicted of took place in August 1961. Two lovers had parked in a wheat field outside London. A gunman surprised them and ordered them to drive down the A6 highway to a rest area, where he murdered the man and then shot the woman after raping her. She, however, survived.

The police soon found a man, Peter Alphon, who fit the woman's description of the assailant. They tied him to the murder weapon and proved his alibi a fabrication. Moreover, Alphon was identified from a lineup by another woman who asserted that two weeks after the first incident, while attempting to rape her, he had shouted out, "I am the A6 killer."

Alphon went unrecognized, however, by the first woman who had survived the shooting in the A6 rest area. She instead identified James Hanratty. When Hanratty was brought to trial he weakened his defense by changing his alibi on the witness stand. The jury found him guilty, and he was hanged six weeks later, in April 1962.

After his execution, supporters found seven reliable witnesses who confirmed his altered alibi. Peter Alphon later confessed to the killing repeatedly: in notes to a friend, in a telephone call to Hanratty's parents, at a press conference in Paris, and in a letter to Britain's Home Secretary. No official action was taken, however. The government seemed determined to leave the embarrassing incident in the past.[1]

Lennon and Ono did their best to raise public awareness of the apparent travesty. On December 11, 1969, at the premiere of Ringo Starr's movie *The Magic Christian*, they unfurled a banner reading "Britain murdered Hanratty." On December 14 they participated in a demonstration at Speakers' Corner in London where Hanratty's father called for an inquiry; then the protestors delivered a petition demanding an official inquiry to 10 Downing Street. On December 15, at a benefit concert in London's Lyceum, Ono began a song by screaming out to the audience, "Britain! You killed Hanratty—you murderer!" Lennon even produced and directed a forty-minute color film on the case, which was screened in St. Martin in the Fields Church in London.[2]

Although their protests coincided with parliamentary passage of a law to end capital punishment in Britain, the hoped-for inquiry never came. Hanratty's supporters doggedly continued to keep the issue alive, and four decades after the conviction and hanging the case was reexamined in the light of the newly developed technology of DNA testing. The results showed with high statistical probability that Hanratty had, after all, committed the crimes. The issue was still not completely resolved, as believers in his innocence maintained that the evidence had been contaminated during the investigative and judicial processes by handlers who had no inkling of what procedures would one day be important to scientific investigators.[3]

Another social issue to which Lennon and Ono devoted their time and energy was racism. One of the most controversial figures in British politics in the late 1960s was Enoch Powell, an opinionated and articulate conservative member of Parliament. Alarmed by the influx of dark-skinned people into Great Britain and what it portended for society, he openly urged that such immigration be stopped and that blacks be sent back to their countries of origin. The alternative to this action, Powell predicted, would be a future race war.

To Lennon, whose life had been completely transformed by a style of music originated by black Americans and who knew talented black musicians and songwriters as friends, Powell's racist proposal was abhorrent. He and Ono decided to support Michael X (Michael Abdul Malik), an articulate black leader who claimed to stand for a nonviolent approach to race relations and modeled himself on America's Malcolm X. A native of Trinidad, Michael operated a cultural center in London called the Black House.[4]

In February 1970, Lennon and Ono staged a media event in which they showed up at the Black House with army-style haircuts. They carried plastic bags containing the shoulder-length hair they had cut off and exchanged it for a pair of bloodstained boxing trunks once worn by Muhammad Ali. They announced they would auction the trunks off and donate the proceeds to peace; Michael X stated he would auction off their famous hair at Sotheby's and donate the money to his "brothers."[5]

Convinced of his good intentions, Lennon and Ono continued to support Michael X even after he was charged with extortion and fled to his native Trinidad to avoid a jail term. He started a commune while there and began lobbying for agrarian reform on the island. Then one day the police found two of his associates buried near his house. He was charged with murder and after a questionable trial was sentenced to be hanged.

Lennon was adamant in his opposition to capital punishment, regardless of the man's guilt or innocence. He sent a letter to influential individuals around the world—to Queen Elizabeth and all members of the royal family, leaders of Parliament, British universities, the London newspapers, and, because Michael X was Muslim, to the heads of all Muslim nations— asking for their help in pressuring the Trinidadian government to commute the death sentence. Lennon's best efforts proved futile; the sentence was carried out.[6]

These were also the years when the South African government grew notorious for its repression of the vast majority of its own citizens under the segregationist policy of apartheid. White South African citizens who traveled around the world for sports or cultural events encountered embarrassing criticism and often sparked demonstrations. When the South African rugby team traveled to Scotland for a match in December 1969, members were greeted with public agitation that resulted in the arrest of ninety-six protestors. Sympathetic to their cause, Lennon paid the fines for the entire group.[7]

He kept up his involvement with social issues even though these were dark days for him personally. He had felt under assault by society ever since leaving his wife for Yoko Ono. Mentally battered by the miscarriage of their child, the estrangement from the other Beatles, the trumped-up drug arrest and conviction, and his relentless excoriation by the media and much of the public, he had taken refuge in heroin. Aware of the danger, he self-rehabilitated. Then he made art out of the process by writing and recording "Cold Turkey."

In March 1970, he was relieved and excited to discover *The Primal Scream* and the drug-free alternative offered by Arthur Janov. But then, shortly after beginning the therapy with Janov, he received the telephone call from Paul McCartney announcing the imminent release of McCartney's solo album and the de facto breakup of the Beatles. This came on top of the collapse of plans for the gargantuan Toronto Peace Festival due to organizational difficulties.

In this context Lennon began a period of radicalization, during which he came to question whether any meaningful change could be achieved without direct confrontation with the establishment. His flirtation with the radical Left began under the tutelage of two of its British representatives, Tariq Ali and Robin Blackburn—who were then editors of the British Marxist journal *Red Mole* and, respectively, the leader of the Vietnam Solidarity Committee and a student leader at the London School of Economics. Lennon would later disparage his own activities during the period: "That radicalism was phony, really, because it was out of guilt. I'd always felt guilty that I made money, so I had to give it away or lose it. I don't mean I was a hypocrite—when I believe, I believe right down to the roots."[8]

In fact, he did carry out the new agenda with his characteristic enthusiasm. Wearing a *Red Mole* tee shirt, he marched with a crowd of fifteen

hundred demonstrators supporting the editors of a counterculture maga-
zine being tried by the government and protesting against British policy in
Northern Ireland. He even carried a placard: "For the IRA, Against British
Imperialism."[9]

He publicly supported the takeover of shipyards in Scotland by eight
thousand laid-off workers. Rather than submit to a cost-saving measure,
they refused to give up their jobs and moved in to occupy the factories.
Lennon contributed a thousand pounds one week to their relief fund.[10]

Most notably, stimulated by an interview he gave to *Red Mole*, he wrote
a song for the movement. "Power to the People," another attempt at an
anthem, became a million seller, but Lennon later denigrated the song's
importance and called it "embarrassing" and written out of a sense of
guilt.[11]

The uniform of a political radical did not fit well on Lennon. While
keenly sensitive to social injustices, he always felt they could be rectified
by improving the system in which they occurred, not by scrapping it. Even
when he promoted extreme positions, his vision was tempered by pragmatism and a dose of humor. When the English press tried to stigmatize him
as being extreme left wing, even Communist, he responded: "They knock
me for saying 'Power to the People' and say that no one section should
have the power. Rubbish. The people aren't a section. The people means
everyone. I think everyone should own everything equally and that the
people should own part of the factories and they should have some say in
who is the boss and who does what. Students should be able to select teachers. . . . The socialism I talk about is British socialism, not where some daft
Russian might do it. That might suit them. Us, we'd have a nice socialism
here, a British socialism."[12]

Conditional radical or not, when Lennon moved to America in August
1971 (primarily a visit to search for Ono's daughter, who was being kept
away from her by ex-husband, Tony Cox) he continued his foray into left-
ist politics. One of the people who read the news of the arrival of Lennon
and Ono was Jerry Rubin. He was in New York with Abbie Hoffman, both
members of the "Chicago Seven"—defendants in the conspiracy trial that
followed the riotous Democratic convention of 1968. Rubin impulsively

called the Apple organization to seek a meeting with John and Yoko and happily discovered that they were interested in meeting him. On the following Saturday afternoon, Rubin and Hoffman met Lennon and Ono in Washington Square Park.

They showed the couple around New York and in coming weeks introduced them to key players in America's radical movement. Over the next two years, Lennon and Ono would meet frequently with Rubin and Hoffman and friends, and they took part in a variety of activities in support of social justice.

In October 1971, while in Syracuse, New York, for a Yoko Ono exhibition at the Everson Museum, they joined a group of Onondaga Indians protesting the government's takeover of land belonging to them in order to build a freeway.[13]

On December 10, at Rubin's request, they headlined a concert in Ann Arbor, Michigan, in support of John Sinclair, who had been sent to jail for ten years for selling two joints of marijuana to an undercover policeman. Sinclair was freed three days later.[14]

Just before Christmas they appeared at Harlem's Apollo Theater in a concert to benefit the families of prisoners who had been shot during the bloody September uprising in New York's Attica Correctional Facility.[15]

In January 1972, Lennon sat in on the trial of the "Harlem Six," black members of a religious group who had been charged with murder, then held in legal limbo—unable to obtain either bail or a trial—for six years.[16]

In early February, he and Ono took part in a demonstration in New York City to show solidarity with the Irish civil rights movement—prompted by the killing the previous weekend of thirteen demonstrators by British troops in Northern Ireland.[17]

In April, the premiere issue of a New Left magazine called *SunDance* contained the first in a projected series of columns written jointly by Lennon and Ono. Their first effort was titled "It's Never Too Late to Start from the Start," an essay dealing with women's liberation.[18]

Under Ono's influence, Lennon had gradually become conscious of his own chauvinistic attitude toward women, the result of being raised in the male-dominant milieu of Liverpool and then enjoying years of female adoration as a rock star. According to this attitude, women existed for sexual gratification, keeping house, and serving tea; nor did Lennon have any deep remorse about physically abusing them. He is reported to have vented his temper on both Cynthia and Yoko.[19] Now, in his thirties, he was finally opening his eyes to the pain he had caused in his blindness. "I used to be cruel to my woman, and physically—any woman," he said in *Playboy* in 1980. "I was a hitter. I couldn't express myself and I hit. I fought men and I hit women. That is why I am always on about peace, you see. It is the most violent people who go for love and peace. . . . But I sincerely believe in love and peace. I am a violent man who has learned not to be violent and regrets his violence. I will have to be a lot older before I can face in public how I treated women as a youngster."[20]

His eyes opened even wider. He became conscious that his own error was just a minuscule part of a much wider problem—that being the systemic consignment of half of the world's population to second-class status. Once awakened, he turned his insight into art.

Recalling a pithy phrase Yoko had once interjected into an interview, he used it as the title of a blistering song about the subject, performed for the first time in May 1972. The title, "Woman Is the Nigger of the World," was so incendiary that few radio stations dared to play the record, and it consequently became the worst-selling of Lennon's solo career. Regardless, he was always proud of it, arguing that he had written the very first song about women's liberation, since it preceded "I Am Woman," the hugely popular record by Helen Reddy.[21]

The views expressed in the lyrics signified a profound shift in Lennon's thought, a rise in consciousness that helped make possible his own mentally liberated commitment as a "househusband" a few years later, in the late seventies. It was one thing to make facile comments about social and political equality in front of a microphone; it was quite another to internalize the concept and actually begin to alter behavior accordingly.

The album that included "Woman Is the Nigger of the World," *Some Time in New York City*, fared no better than the single. It featured the unabashedly political songs Lennon and Ono had been writing since moving to America. Tracks included "John Sinclair," "Attica State," "Sisters,

O Sisters," "Angela" (about Berkeley radical Angela Davis), and two songs about the Irish problem, "Luck of the Irish" and "Sunday Bloody Sunday" (a reaction to the killing of thirteen Irish demonstrators by British troops on January 30, 1972).[22]

Ever since his experiences with Primal Scream therapy, Lennon had made a conscious effort to keep his music and lyrics direct and stripped of artifice. Gone were the days of surreal lyrics and ornate musical accompaniment epitomized by "I Am the Walrus"; he wanted to communicate in the simplest way possible, harking back to the early days of rock 'n' roll. In the songs he had been writing in America, he wanted to project the feeling that they were reports on the day's news. In fact, the sleeve design for *Some Time in New York City* mimicked a newspaper, with headlines and columns.

He paid a price for that directness. To many listeners his new approach ended up sounding like preachiness and hectoring. Where was the poetry? The finesse? Why had one of the world's most brilliant songwriters degenerated into churning out political tirades? The album was both a critical and a commercial failure.

He also paid a price for his strident positions and his association with radicals. Mingled among the audience members the night he performed at the Ann Arbor rally in support of John Sinclair were informants for the Federal Bureau of Investigation. A file was opened on him, spelling things out so that even the ossified J. Edgar Hoover could understand: "Source advised approximately five well known rock bands and/or singers performed at the rally, including John Lennon and wife Yoko Ono. Lennon formerly with group known as the Beatles."[23]

In late January 1972, Lennon donated $75,000 to help with the expenses of his friends in the New Left, and this worrying intelligence prompted an urgent coded teletype to J. Edgar Hoover from the bureau's New York office.[24] In February, Senator Strom Thurmond received a memorandum from the staff of his Senate Judiciary Committee apprizing him of John Lennon's support of members of the Chicago Seven and their intention to use him to promote the disruption of the 1972 Republican National Convention the same way they had disrupted the 1968 Democratic National

Convention. The memo included a suggestion that the almost inevitable outcome could be avoided by the simple expedient of revoking the visa that allowed Lennon to remain in the United States.[25]

Thurmond agreed and forwarded the memo to Attorney General John Mitchell and the White House. On March 6, 1972, the Immigration and Naturalization Service terminated Lennon's visa and started deportation proceedings.

For more than four years afterward, Lennon would struggle to remain in the United States. During that time the FBI subjected him to surveillance in the form of wiretaps that were secret and personal observation that was often deliberately overt.[26]

The government feared the prospect of a violent confrontation at the Republican convention that would taint the event and impact the reelection chances of Richard Nixon. An early meeting of the radical group seemed to underscore that possibility. A strategy emerged that featured a series of concerts around the country to arouse young people politically, with the goal of a million-person demonstration outside the convention headquarters in San Diego (the venue was later moved to Miami).

Lennon and Ono completely shared the New Left's hatred of Nixon and its objective of getting him out of power. But they rejected the means Jerry Rubin and his associates proposed. Speaking for himself and Ono, Lennon explained in a 1980 *Playboy* interview:

> Yeah, it was "We'll help with the concert, we'll sing our part." We were naive, as well, thinking none of the money would go to anything nasty. . . .
>
> The infamous San Diego meeting that got us into all the immigration problems was really a nonexistent situation. [We had] this so-called meeting with Jerry, Abbie, Allen Ginsberg, John Sinclair . . . where they were trying to get us to go to the San Diego Republican Convention. When they described their plans, we just kept looking at each other. It was the poets and the straight politicals divided. Ginsberg was with us. He kept saying, "What are we trying to do, create another Chicago?" That's what they wanted. We said, "We ain't buying this. We're not going to draw children into a situation to create violence—so you can overthrow *what?*—and replace it with *what?*"[27]

The radicals' strategy was not implemented, and the hoped-for demonstration never took place. When the FBI's files on Lennon were finally declassified and then released to the public in 1997—after fourteen years of litigation by historian Jon Wiener and the American Civil Liberties Union—they revealed Lennon's refusal to compromise his pacifist principles. An FBI informant wrote that Lennon provisionally agreed to come to the demonstrations at the convention if his attendance could be unannounced and if they were "peaceful." Another document stated that a person, whose name was withheld, "had numerous conversations with John Lennon and his wife about becoming active in the New Left movement in the United States and that Lennon and his wife seem uninterested."[28]

The whole episode proved to be simply a reaffirmation of the wisdom of cynicism—regarding the motivations not only of radical leaders but those of our trusted government officials as well. The FBI rightly worried that Lennon had the influence and the inclination to mobilize youth against the president and the Vietnam War, but that is not illegal activity. As Jon Wiener notes, "It's true that he spoke out against the war at rallies and demonstrations. But the files contain no evidence that Lennon committed any criminal acts: no bombings, no terrorism, no conspiracies. His activities were precisely the kind protected by the First Amendment, which is not limited to U.S. citizens."[29]

To keep from acknowledging their inappropriate and fruitless surveillance, the FBI fought for years to keep many pounds of documentation out of reach of the public who paid its salaries. Two of the documents the government fought with great tenacity to keep classified are illuminating. One featured the lyrics to Lennon's song "John Sinclair." These had been printed on the back of his album *Some Time in New York City* and thus were available to the public ten years before litigation began. Another summarized an informant's 1972 visit to New York City. There she met a girl named Linda who had a parrot trained to shout "Right on!" whenever the conversation got rousing.[30]

Ultimately, the FBI chose to release most of the documents and settle the case out of court rather than permit testimony under oath by two agents who had supervised the Lennon investigation. In 1980, in another case, one of these agents had been convicted and the other was named as an unindicted coconspirator for conspiring to violate individuals' civil rights by authorizing break-ins and searches of suspects' homes.[31]

As for his struggle with the Immigration and Naturalization Service, Lennon had to go to court repeatedly to contest the attempt to deport him. He finally won permanent residency in the United States only after it became clear that he had been subject to a personal vendetta by Attorney General John Mitchell (the same John Mitchell who served prison time for conspiracy, obstruction of justice, and perjury during the Watergate scandal).[32]

Lennon's dalliance with the New Left effectively ended on election night in 1972, when Richard Nixon scored one of the biggest landslides in United States presidential history. Suddenly it became clear that the "revolutionary movement" Lennon had supported was nothing but a blustery wind passing across the political landscape, that momentum for social upheaval had dissipated, and that the pressure and harassment he was feeling from the establishment would only increase. As the unwelcome election returns began to come in, he started taking drugs and the pent-up disappointment and anger spilled over into his relations with Yoko.[33]

"Life doesn't imitate art; *Life is art*," Lennon would later maintain.[34] He and Ono had committed to transforming their relationship into an ongoing work of art, aimed at exploring the potential of their joint imagination. But great art is never linear; it is made real by the unanticipated, profound by ambiguities, and truthful by human weaknesses. Though they passed several more months together on the trajectory they had established, the bond holding their relationship together started to crumble on that night in November and Lennon began the descent into the bleakest depths of his long, dark night.

In October 1973, he publicly separated from Ono, flew to Los Angeles, and began what he subsequently referred to as his "lost weekend." In the 1945 film of that name, Ray Milland goes on a drunken, out-of-control tour of hell that lasts for a weekend. Lennon's would last for fifteen months.

For Lennon, it was a second chance at the liberty of his youth— a boundless freedom he had not felt completely since the day Brian

Epstein persuaded him to wear a suit on stage and began to package him as a commodity. He plunged into the adventure with relish, exhilarated by the absence of constraints. Unfortunately, though, he quickly fell into a self-destructive pattern of liquor, drugs, and parties.

Yes, he was an irresponsible teenager again, but he was a teenager who possessed the maturity of a thirty-something. He soon realized that freedom without a foundation is an abyss.

Within days after arriving in California, Lennon was beginning to understand the gravity of his decision to separate from Ono. Elliot Mintz, a mutual friend of John and Yoko who lived in Los Angeles, said, "The excitement of being on his own in L.A. seemed to me to last about a week. After that a sadness set in, and it never got better. It got progressively worse. His main ambition was getting back to Yoko."[35] She, however, was in no rush to patch up the rift. She wanted Lennon to remain in California until he had absolutely no doubts that he preferred to live with her in a stable relationship.

As month piled upon month, Lennon became more dissatisfied and anxious and bitter, speaking recklessly, creating disturbances, getting thrown out of nightclubs, lashing out physically at others. Mintz described the situation: "He was a miserable drunk. One brandy Alexander and he was absolutely delightful. Two was OK. Three, and he started snarling."[36]

Hoping to stabilize himself through work, he created two albums of his own during the separation, as well as producing one for his friend Harry Nilsson. *Rock 'n' Roll* documented Lennon's nostalgia for the days of his youth. He performed cover versions of such classics as Gene Vincent's "Be-Bop-A-Lula"—a song he performed on stage the day he met Paul McCartney. *Walls and Bridges* included songs addressed to Yoko Ono in which he declared musically that he was ready to come back. The album sold a million copies and climbed to the top of the charts, but Lennon saw it through different eyes: "It gives off an aura of misery. Because I was miserable."[37]

The beginning of their reconciliation came on Thanksgiving Day, 1974. Elton John had helped Lennon during the recording of *Walls and Bridges*, playing piano and adding vocal backing for "Whatever Gets You thru the Night." He assured Lennon that though Lennon considered this song his

:yle their relationship developed into—Ono being the bread-
ennon being a househusband—Lennon admitted in a *Play-*
: "It saved my life. . . . I was stuck in the feeling that one did
justified in being alive unless one was fulfilling other people's
her they were contractual dreams or the public's dreams, or
own dreams and illusions about what I thought I was *sup-*
hich, in retrospect, turned out to not be what I am."[1]

is adult life John Lennon had been simultaneously perpetu-
ing to live up to the legend of "John Lennon." The superstar-
ius role dictated the behavior of the man, who felt obligated
the fictional character's agenda. How can someone acknowl-
perstar-crusader-genius *not* strive to be the person everyone

ey to his escape had been linking up with Yoko Ono, who
m not as a legend but as a person. Another had been Primal
apy, which pried the lid off his deepest insecurities and engen-
onesty. The final key had been the lost weekend, which tanta-
th freedom, then coldly drove home the point that the price of
John Lennon" would be Faustian.

he point. He turned his back on the illusion and the inauthen-
resented. He concentrated on his relationship with Yoko Ono,
ely with his son. "If I can't deal with a child, I can't deal with
o matter what artistic gains I get, or how many gold records, if
a success out of my relationship with the people I supposedly
verything else is bullshit."[2]

possessed the unique qualities that had made John Lennon a
e, but now he determined to bring them under his control, not
The hardest thing is facing yourself. It's easier to shout 'Revo-
'Power to the people' than it is to look at yourself and try to find
eal inside you and what isn't, when you're pulling the wool over
yes. That's the hardest one."[3]

fter a break of five years, he finally began to create music again,
ote a song about and for Sean, "Beautiful Boy (Darling Boy)."
imple observations of daily life with a child and evocative hints

least favorite on the album it would go all the way to the top of the American music charts. Lennon, who had never recorded a single as a solo artist
that had reached number one in America, expressed doubt. Elton John
challenged him—if it did, would he promise to return the favor by appearing on stage in one of Elton's shows?[38]

"Whatever Gets You thru the Night" reached number one in mid-
November 1974, and the promise was fulfilled in a concert at Madison
Square Garden on Thanksgiving evening, when Lennon, to a tumultuous
response from the audience, came out to join Elton on three songs. What
Elton knew, and Lennon didn't, was that Yoko Ono was in the audience.

Lennon recalled: "She was backstage afterward, and there was just
that moment when we saw each other and like, it's like in the movies,
you know, when time stands still? And there was silence, everything went
silent, y'know, and we were just sort of lookin' at each other."[39] Six weeks
later, in January 1975, Lennon moved back in with her permanently.

1

HOUSEH

On October 9, 1975—nine m
began living together again,
fifth birthday—Yoko gave bi
all the remarkable convolutions of Joh
he now embarked was arguably the m
achieved international renown by the a
defined his generation, expanded his con
and meditation, rankled bigots, prudes,
by his freethinking behavior, ennobled l
humiliated himself in debauchery—this
sonas, but all of them in the limelight, n
completely so that he could devote hims

His stated purpose was to take perso
into the boy's mind and body during his
his model the Catholic Church, which u
the first five to seven years, it could guara
would become.

Those who had dismissed Lennon's "W
insights as liberal posturing were dumbfc
cho superstar really meant it. He committ
Ono displayed an aptitude for financial an
responsibilities to her and assumed the ro
to women—taking care of Sean's daily nee

Of the life
winner and
boy intervie
not—was no
dreams, whe
fulfilling my
posed to be,

For all of
ating and tr
crusader-ge
to carry out
edged as a s
expects?

The first
related to h
Scream the
dered raw l
lized him w
remaining

He took
tic life it re
and ultima
anything. I
I can't mal
love, then

He still
world figu
vice versa.
lution' and
out what's
your own

When,
Lennon w
Amid the

of fatherly love, he included a wonderful piece of wisdom, an aphorism expressing perfectly his Zen-like clarity about the danger of being illusion directed: "Life is what happens to you while you're busy making other plans."

The liberated John Lennon found authentication in domesticity and in being the father he never had. In the past he had customarily stayed in bed until after noon. Now he arose early every morning and fed Sean his breakfast, often preparing it himself. He structured his life around Sean's meals and naps, drinking coffee and reading newspapers or books for a while when he had free time, then getting up to cook or to supervise the next meal, making sure that Sean received balanced nutrition and no sweets. He read children's books to the boy, made sure that he had stimulating toys to play with, and regulated his television viewing, emphasizing commercial-free educational programs such as *Sesame Street*. He suffered through the inevitable tantrums, and as the boy grew older Lennon took him for carriage rides around Central Park and walks around the city.

The minutia of home life brought him unexpected satisfaction. When he baked his first loaf of bread, he was so excited and proud that he took Polaroid photographs of it and sent one to a friend in Los Angeles via special messenger. He compared his domestic adventure to withdrawing from the world and living in a monastery, and the mastery of baking bread to a Zen experience.[4]

His househusband experiences gave him a firsthand education about the daily life of housewives.

I'll say to all housewives, I now understand what they're screaming about. Because . . . what I'm describing is most women's lives. . . . That's what I've been doing for five years. . . . I was being just like a million, a hundred million people who are mainly female, I just went from meal to meal. Is he well? Has he brushed his teeth? Has he eaten enough vegetables? Is he overeating? Am I limiting his diet too much? Did he get some goodies? What condition is the child in? How is she when she comes back from the office? Is she going to talk to me or is she just going to talk about business?[5]

He now understood, but he also understood that most women had it worse. What percentage of housewives enjoyed the luxury, as he did, of a nanny, an assistant, and a housecleaner? And when he took over cooking duties, it was by choice and for his own satisfaction, whereas most women who managed the home for a family *had* to cook three meals a day.

No marriage is totally harmonious, and his renewed relationship with Yoko Ono was not without tensions, but he started over with greater maturity and a broader perspective. He began to understand that any relationship has its ups and downs, with critical points that must be worked through. It may appear to be a simple solution to walk away from a relationship that is in crisis, but the sad truth is that the person who walks away will have to face the same kinds of painful decisions in the next relationship that comes along. An even sadder truth is that the next relationship might not equal the one given up. "When I was kicked out," he told *Playboy* in 1980, "I realized where I was, which was on a raft in the middle of the universe, and whatever happened, presuming I could have started another relationship, I would have ended up in the same place—*if I was lucky*. And that's a big *if*."[6] In the same interview, Lennon drew on the Hindu concept of karma to express his thoughts about the ebb-and-flow of personal relationships.

> It's like what they say about karma. If you don't get it right in this lifetime, you have to come back and go through it again. Well, those laws that are sort of cosmically talked about, accepted or not but talked about, apply down to the most minute detail of life, too. It's like "Instant Karma," which is my way of saying it, right? It's not just some big cosmic thing, although it's that as well, but it's also the small things, like your life here and your relationship with the person you want to live with and be with.[7]

In other words, individuals in their daily lives are subject to the same laws as the cosmos. Those involved in a challenging relationship can face up to the challenge and grow as a result of the experience, or they can postpone the lesson to another day and confront it in some future relationship. Regardless, the lesson must be learned.

From 1976 until mid-1980, Lennon and Ono worked on their relationship within the framework of the reversed breadwinner/housekeeper roles. While he concentrated on Sean's upbringing, she represented him at official meetings and invested their income—primarily royalties from his music—in real estate, dairy cattle, and Egyptian antiquities. For diversion, they savored life in Manhattan and took family vacations to such destinations as Long Island, Palm Beach, and Disney World, as well as to Japan for several months at a time.

Lennon also took solo jaunts to such places as Hong Kong, Singapore, and South Africa at Ono's suggestion, based on the advice she was given by her psychic advisors, numerologists, and "direction people." Despite his skepticism regarding supernatural beings, Lennon was fascinated with what he labeled magic—that is, utilization of the omnipresent "power" that he equated with God and that he thought would one day be understood scientifically—and he respected Ono's apparent intuitive grasp of it.

He was not the only one she convinced. Family friend Elliot Mintz commented: "If she were to say, 'I think it's important for you to travel in a northwesterly direction for approximately eighteen thousand miles tomorrow morning,' that would be enough. She has said those things to me and I have done them. She would say, if you do this, it's going to dramatically alter the next six months of your life in a favorable way. There were direction moves that she gave me that did significantly alter the structure of my life."

Mintz also became convinced that Yoko Ono was psychic. "I'm a fairly pragmatic guy and consider myself to be a realist. But I am now a believer in her abilities. She *is* telepathic. I do know that. I do know she reads minds."[8]

Perhaps Lennon found enough evidence of the validity of her insights to be comfortable following her instructions. Perhaps his habitually open mind, which had betrayed him before with such figures as the Maharishi, was simply beguiled by Yoko Ono's self-confident self-deceptions. Perhaps he was so grateful for the second chance she gave him to establish a psychologically grounding relationship that he humored her. Whatever the truth, he did enjoy five years of relative contentment.

With their domestic life taking so much of their time, the two became almost invisible in the worlds of art and music. However, Lennon was not then creatively idle. His largest project was a book in the same vein as *In His Own Write* and *A Spaniard in the Works*. Titled *Skywriting by Word of Mouth*, it was ultimately published posthumously. The book incorporated an autobiographical sketch he wrote about his relationship with Ono for a musical to be called *The Ballad of John and Yoko*. He also wrote a play, poetry, and drafts and fragments of several songs, created more than a hundred drawings, and made from twenty to thirty visual collages—fashioned from shapes and figures taken from magazines—as well as a number of sound collages ("mind movies") he recorded on tape.[9]

None of this creative work was shared with anyone other than close friends, though several of the song fragments were reworked and expanded to appear on the *Double Fantasy* album, and two demo tapes were used in 1995 as the foundation for "Free as a Bird" and "Real Love," new records by the reconstituted Beatles.

Because of their stature as one of the world's most newsworthy couples, the protracted absence of Lennon and Ono from the public arena aroused great curiosity. They responded in May 1979 by writing an open letter to the public, published as a paid advertisement in newspapers in New York, London, and Tokyo. Titled "A Love Letter from John and Yoko to People Who Ask Us What, When, and Why," it was ostensibly to let people know what they were doing. However, it was not so much a glimpse of *what* they were doing as *how* they were approaching life as a "new clear" family and their contentment with their lifestyle.

The letter provided fascinating insights into their thinking. In describing their technique for dealing with a person who was angry with them, the John Lennon of the "All You Need Is Love" era was still very much in evidence: "We draw a halo around his or her head in our minds. Does the person stop being angry then? Well, we don't know! We know, though, that when we draw a halo around a person, suddenly the person starts to look like an angel to us."[10]

When the couple finally returned to the public eye in late 1980, they were barraged with questions about the reason for the hiatus. Lennon summed up his perspective in simple language reminiscent of his comments about the value of meditation for creativity ("You can't paint a picture on dirty paper; you need a clean sheet"). He told *Playboy*:

> You breathe in and you breathe out. We breathed in after breathing out for a long time. The *I Ching* calls it sitting still. A lot more can happen when you're not doing anything than when you appear to be doing something. Although it looks that what John and Yoko were doing for five years was not doing anything, we were doing a hell of a lot. Sitting still is one way of describing it. Sitting still, amazing things happen, you see. And now we're not sitting still. Now we're moving around. And maybe in a few years we'll sit still again. Because life is long, I presume.
>
> So now we are breathing out. One must do both: One withdraws, one expands; tide in, tide out. It's better to breathe in and breathe out rather than just always trying to breathe out. You can run out of breath.[11]

Lennon's primary stimulus for the beginning of a "breathing out" phase was a dramatic experience at sea. Perhaps from childhood imaginings of his seaman father, he had always been captivated by the idea of sailing the ocean. He took lessons in early 1980, and in June he chartered a forty-one-foot schooner to voyage from Rhode Island to Bermuda—three thousand miles in seven days. Once beyond the sight of land he felt the freedom of the open sea. Farther out into the Atlantic, however, he experienced the anxiety that often lurks in freedom's shadow. The schooner encountered a squall that would last for three days. He described what happened next in *Playboy*. Unexpectedly, the captain and his two cousins—everyone on the boat except Lennon—became nauseated.

> They were sick and throwing up and the captain says to me, "There's a storm coming up. Do you want to take over the wheel?" I said, "Do you think I can?" I was supposed to be the cabin boy learning the trade, but he said, "Well, you have to. There's no one else who can do it." I said, "Well, you had better keep an eye on me." He said he would.
>
> Five minutes later he goes down below to sleep and says, "See you later."

Strong winds and high waves pummeled the small craft. Lennon held to the wheel, never experiencing the nausea that affected everyone else— a benefit of his fish-and-rice diet. He continued:

No one else could move. They were sick as dogs. So I was there, driving the boat, for six hours, keeping it on course. I was buried under water. I was smashed in the face by waves for six solid hours. It won't go away. You can't change your mind. It's like being on stage—once you're on, there's no gettin' off.

A couple of the waves had me on my knees. I was just hanging on with my hands on the wheel . . . and I was having the time of my life! I was screaming sea chanteys and shoutin' at the gods! . . .

I arrived in Bermuda . . . so centered after the experience at sea that I was tuned in, or whatever, to the cosmos. And all these songs came![12]

The floodgates opened on his creativity, and his sabbatical as a house-husband came to an end. Over the next few weeks he wrote (or reworked and finished from earlier fragments) all the songs that would appear on his final collaborative albums with Yoko Ono, *Double Fantasy* and the posthumous *Milk and Honey*.[13]

One song in particular voiced Lennon's feelings about his five-year withdrawal from the public arena. He addressed it to the people who had chided him about his long absence. His reclusiveness irritated many people who lived vicariously through him and Ono, people who had come to expect their commitment to certain causes and regular coverage of their exploits in the news, people who seemed to feel that they knew better than Lennon what was in his best interests and did not hesitate to tender advice. The old John Lennon would have lacerated them with sarcasm, but he had grown more philosophical. He addressed them instead with amused detachment, as someone no longer on the merry-go-round.

In "Watching the Wheels," Buddha has come to Manhattan. He settles down on the sidewalk along Central Park, assuming the lotus position. Some passersby call him crazy, some lazy. Some give him warnings, others try to enlighten him. Surely he can't be happy, they're all convinced, since he's not taking part in their game.

Perhaps, but *they* are the ones rushing their lives away, immersed in the illusion. He is content with the role of just sitting there, observing.

Lennon responded to an interviewer's question about the song with language suggestive of some hip Liverpudlian Siddhartha: "Watching the wheels? . . . Wheels go round and round. They're my own wheels, mainly. But, you know, watching meself is like watching everybody else. And I watch meself through my child, too. Then, in a way, nothing is real, if you break the word down. As the Hindus or Buddhists say, it's an illusion, meaning all matter is floating atoms, right? It's Rashomon. We all see it, but the agreed-upon illusion is what we live in."[14]

From his early twenties, Lennon had been living at a furious pace. He was a gifted person and he accomplished extraordinary things, but he finally came to understand that he had climbed onto a merry-go-round of illusion and that every day he focused on trying to be "John Lennon" he sacrificed another part of himself. In time he realized he was caught up in a hopeless quest. He had only one choice—to let it all go.

True to his first principle, independence, he simply got off the ride. Let the world think what it would.

His last five years were spent as a mentally liberated, mature man. Not a man who had fully overcome his demons and his weaknesses, but a man who drew strength from his family relationships. Not a man who no longer had aspirations, but a man who knew the importance of pausing to savor the simple pleasures of life.

Then he died, abruptly, prematurely—but not before completing the work of art he had been creating for more than a decade. Fittingly, it was a fully realized self-portrait.

Suggested Listening
"Give Peace a Chance"
"Beautiful Boy (Darling Boy)"
"Watching the Wheels"

PART FOUR

CYNICAL IDEALISM

12

SUPERSTARS

In 1970, John Lennon commented to an interviewer: "That's been my *hangup*, continually trying to be *Shakespeare* or whatever it is. That's what I'm doing. . . . I'm not competing meself against Elvis. . . . I'm in the game of *all* those things. Of *concept* and *philosophy*, and *ways* of *life*, and *whole movements* in *history*. . . . I'm interested in producing—expressing myself, like they [Shakespeare, Van Gogh, etc.] expressed it, that will mean something to people in any country, in any language, and at any time in history."[1]

On another occasion, he was more articulate and more concise. "If it was another age I would be called a philosopher."[2] Lennon did not leave behind a grand philosophical project along the lines of Aristotle, Kant, Hegel, Wittgenstein, or Sartre. However, he did leave an impressive body of creative work and two decades of interviews. From them the outlines of his philosophy can be sketched.

Fundamentally, he stood for a human-centered approach to daily life and world affairs. God is not some individualized entity to be worshiped and counted on for assistance but "a concept by which we measure our pain." He/She/It is not an all-powerful being representing what is good in the universe but a nebulous background force, a "powerhouse," a neutral source of energy that can be employed for good or ill.

Lennon did not think of himself as a religious man, except in a humanistic way that would satisfy very few believers. When asked directly if he would call himself religious, he first responded, "I wouldn't really."

Then the interviewer stretched the word to mean being "concerned," as the Protestant theologian Paul Tillich had put it, and Lennon changed his answer: "Well, I am then. I'm concerned alright. I'm concerned with people."[3]

Lennon believed that humanity could reach a higher plane, that average men and women had it in their power to help reshape their culture in that direction if only they would recognize that capability. He devoted considerable effort to trying to make them aware of their power.

He may have failed to bring his ideal society into existence, but Lennon never gave up his convictions that love ought to be the binding force in society and that peace was the goal toward which the world should be striving. "I am not in the group of people who think that, because all our dreams didn't come true in the sixties, everything we said was invalid. There isn't any peace in the world despite our efforts, but I still believe the hippie peace-and-love thing was worthwhile. . . . If somebody stands up and smiles and then gets smacked in the face, that smack doesn't invalidate the smile. It existed."[4]

Love, of course, was an encompassing term meant to convey a range of benign emotions toward our fellow human beings—not just affection but concern, sympathy, readiness to forgive, etc.—which, if displayed daily, would create the kind of harmonious and supportive environment we all long to discover: Shangri-la.

As he suggested in "All You Need Is Love," Lennon believed that the key to achieving this state of affairs is self-transformation. The one thing each of us can do that absolutely no one else has the ability to do is change ourselves. While that may sound trite, consider how few people make a sincere and successful attempt to do so. If we, too, hunger for Lennon's harmonious and peaceful world, we can always choose to alter our daily behavior and choose to take difficult stands we now avoid; that is, we have it in our power *personally* to impact the world in a positive way.

Lennon's point was that the more people who can be persuaded to attempt self-transformation, the better our society will become. He was in good company. Gandhi had said, "We need to be the change we wish to see in the world."[5]

One proven method of self-transformation is through meditation, a discipline Lennon acquired under the Maharishi and continued to respect for the remainder of his life because of its practical benefits. Practitioners have known for thousands of years that *something* beneficial occurs as a result of regular meditation. Recent scientific research has confirmed the effects and started to explain how they come about.

Studies have shown that in the meditating brain, activity is redirected from the right hemisphere of the prefrontal cortex to the left—a shift that appears to reorient the brain from a fight-or-flight stress mode to one of acceptance and contentment. This shift has been demonstrated in other studies to enhance the immune system as well as significantly reduce blood pressure. Moreover, research suggests that meditation can actually "reset" the brain—raising the threshold at which it becomes aware of and affected by stress.[6]

Lennon found it therapeutic to still the conscious mind and slip out of day-to-day preoccupations. Not only did meditation soothe his nervous system and regenerate his creativity, it kept him aware of the illusory nature of everyday "reality." ("All matter is floating atoms, right? It's Rashomon. We all see it, but the agreed-upon illusion is what we live in.")[7]

However, he was no Buddha. (Or perhaps he was a Buddha we can all relate to, with human emotions.) Though idealistic and well intentioned, Lennon had a temper—and he could be exasperated by the disingenuous attitudes of experts and authorities. All of his life he remained on a quest to dig down to fundamental truths, and when the cynic in him encountered layers of duplicity and hypocrisy, he could respond with venom. (Just listen to "Gimme Some Truth.")

In essence, John Lennon was a cynical idealist. He understood the innate self-interest that hobbles our progress toward a better world, but he never lacked optimism that we would get there if we kept our dream in focus. As a philosopher he kept encouraging us to gaze at the horizon; as an artist he felt free to vent his frustration about our dogged myopia.

Shangri-la is not a realm many of us expect to see in our lifetimes, and Lennon's hopeful outlook will always be classified as naive by anyone who ranks Niccolò Machiavelli among history's great thinkers. But if Lennon was naive, he was naive in the same purposeful way as Buddha, Jesus, and Gandhi. How much improvement in this world has been achieved by calculating individuals acting in their own self-interest, and how much by idealistic people acting for the greater good?

If only Lennon had chosen to live in a large tub on the edge of town and make do with one set of clothes, the most famous Cynic, Diogenes, would have been justifiably proud of his philosophical heir. In Lennon he would recognize a fellow citizen of the world, someone who didn't feel bound by social norms, someone willing to suffer condemnation by millions of people to live in accord with his own convictions, someone renowned for his wit, someone who had the audacity to return a medal to his monarch accompanied by a whimsical note. Diogenes might even grudgingly have subscribed to Lennon's idealism, which had nothing to do with Plato's theory of forms and everything to do with moving beyond human pettiness and living up to the potential of our species.

In the ideal world Lennon proposed, people would forgo violence and act out of sympathy and love. They would recognize that such traditional classifiers as religion, nationality, and skin color are meaningless from a cosmic perspective and that any other person should be treated simply as a fellow human being. They would also understand that gender roles are primarily culturally acquired and subject to modification.

Further, they would be content to share material wealth and the earth's resources in the interest of having a milieu of social harmony within which to explore the potential of their own lives. While Lennon remained open-minded about the possibility of life after death, he made his point of focus the here and now—how we can best use the quantum of time chance has allotted to us and what we can achieve as individuals and societies while we are still alive.

He was not dogmatic about the path. In 1980 he said to *Playboy*: "It is unfortunate when people say, 'This is the only way.' That's the only thing I've got against anybody, if they are saying, 'This is the only answer.' I don't want to hear about that. There isn't one answer to anything."[8]

However, he thought it essential that each individual question authority and reach his or her own conclusions. In his mind, too many people subconsciously allowed their parents to retain a stranglehold over their thinking—into middle age and perhaps for all of their lives. This was a regrettable condition for independent adults, one he had been spared because of his fractured relationship with his mother and father.

Each individual has the right and the obligation to make up his or her mind about the path to follow. Having done that, why not think of our existence as an adventure? Some of us have more resources and advantages, some fewer, but each of us has the liberty to use them however we decide. Why settle for an undirected life? Why not consciously make of it a work of art?

For Lennon that meant choosing to work in tandem with Yoko Ono to advance the cause of world peace and promote social, political, and economic justice, as well as to express himself in his music, films, writing, and drawing. For someone with other talents, the canvas might be painted in an entirely different way, but it would be equally valid because it involved living with verve and striving to fulfill potential. An interviewer once challenged him: "You say everybody is equal, but some people are more equal than others." Lennon shot back: "But they are all infinite. They all have infinite possibilities, my friend."[9]

Hand in hand with limitless individual opportunity went personal responsibility. As he told *Playboy* in 1980:

Produce your own dream. If you want to save Peru, go save Peru. It's quite possible to do anything, but not if you put it on the leaders. . . . Don't expect Carter or Reagan or John Lennon or Yoko Ono or Bob Dylan or Jesus Christ to come and do it for you. You have to do it yourself.

That's what the great masters and mistresses have been saying ever since time began. They can point the way, leave signposts and little instructions in various books that are now called holy and worshiped for the cover of the book and not what it says, but the instructions are all there for all to see, have always been and always will be. . . . And people cannot provide it for you. I can't wake you up. *You* can wake you up. I can't cure you. *You* can cure you.[10]

Lennon was emphatic about declaring independence from leaders. "I just believe that leaders and father figures are the mistakes of all the generations before us, and we can't rely on Nixon or on Jesus or whoever we tend to rely on. It's just a lack of responsibility that you expect somebody else to do it. It's, 'Oh, he must help me, and if he doesn't help me, we kill him, or we vote him out.' I think that's the mistake, just having father figures."[11]

To refine the point, Lennon thought that there is nothing wrong with learning from leaders who have something useful to offer, but that after we learn we should function independently. Otherwise, what good is personal independence? What good is free will? He said in a *Playboy* interview: "Arthur Janov accidentally discovered his thing. Before that, he's a straight Freudian psychologist. He finds this screaming by accident and now he's writing theories, books, God knows what about it. If Janov's thing ever got as big as Christianity and then he died, they're going to be worshiping Janov. Not to take away from Janov's or Werner Erhard's or whoever's system or method of learning to swim. . . . Maybe they had a nice way of swimming, but the swimming is the point."[12]

Once we have learned to swim, what then? One of Lennon's primary postulates is that every individual represents a singularity of potential, each having the power to influence others and therefore to help make the world a better place.

The view that every person's actions have a ripple effect on the rest of humanity lies at the heart of his song "Instant Karma (We All Shine On)." Tailoring the Hindu concept of karma to the here and now, he maintains that the cosmic laws of balance and consequences also apply in our current lives and relationships.

If we approach the world as self-gratifying, inconsiderate, spiteful people, how will others react to us? If enough of us decide to be the same way, what kind of society will we have? We need to be mindful of our actions and their consequences. The thinking is reminiscent of Lennon's subtext in "All You Need Is Love"—one person's loving attitude can influence those around him or her, promoting their positive behavior in relations with others, and on ad infinitum.

"Instant Karma (We All Shine On)" erupted from Lennon in a creative burst, in much the same manner as he came up with "Nowhere Man." He awoke the morning of January 27, 1970, with the concept in mind. Before the inspiration could fade, he worked out much of the melody and lyrics. Then he scheduled an impromptu recording session for that evening. Phil Spector, who happened to be in London, was invited to produce. Twelve hours from the moment of its inception, the finished song was on tape.[13]

In the song, Lennon makes an object lesson out of the ridicule he and Yoko Ono have been enduring for their campaign to spread love and peace. His target: the typical skeptic who simply fails to get what they are attempting to do and rejects it out of hand.

Lennon asks what can possibly be going through such a person's mind—"laughing in the face of love." In effect, the skeptic is rejecting a society everyone wants to see and accepting a society rife with pain and fear. Lennon sets up what sounds like a sarcastic comment about the person's arrogant self-importance—does he think of himself as some kind of superstar?—then twists the metaphor in an unexpected direction: "Well, right you are." Think about it, he hints, attempting to raise the person's consciousness.

Instead of accepting and therefore defending things the way they stand, Lennon says, why not consider the alternative of living in a world where pain and fear are mitigated through brotherly love?

But more than simply considering it . . .

If, as Lennon suggests, every person is a "superstar"—that is to say, a beacon whose light spreads out infinitely—then not only does every person bear responsibility for some portion of society's condition, every person has the opportunity to improve it. Even skeptics. "Yeah you," Lennon adds, for those who *still* don't understand where the finger is pointing.

Three years later, Lennon would stumble upon and ultimately promote a technique with the potential to help bring about the world he and other idealists wanted to see.

13

MIND GAMES

Consider the pieces of decorated paper in your wallet that give you the power to walk into a shop you've never visited before and leave with whatever strikes your fancy. Consider how traffic laws are observed on a normal day in the city versus how they are observed while a riot is taking place. Consider how you behave when surrounded by thoughtful, polite people but how petty you would become if marooned somewhere with a group of self-gratifying, devious individuals.

Human society is founded on agreement. Paper money has power only as long as everyone agrees on its value. Laws are relevant only as long as a significant percentage of people agree to observe them. Each of us has a set of values we find valid, but if the group surrounding us is playing by a different set of rules, we'll find it extremely difficult to resist conforming.

What we agree on shapes society. Once enough of us agree that character is more important than skin color, racism will tend to vanish. Once enough of us agree that it is absurd to pay a woman and a man different wages for performing the same job, gender bias will tend to wither away. Once enough of us agree that cigarette smoke is harmful, the acceptability of smoking will tend to diminish.

Now, what if a significant number of us were to agree that—starting next Monday—we would treat *everyone* we encountered with respect, compassion, and love?

John Lennon realized, then propounded, that since as humans we have the ability to change our own habits and convictions, the only barrier to our living in a better world is agreement that we are committed to it. He implied the concept in "All You Need Is Love," "Instant Karma (We All Shine On)," and "Happy Xmas (War Is Over)." However, he crystallized his point of view in his masterpiece, "Imagine." In simple but resonating lyrics, he sketched the framework of a harmonious world he and other dreamers had in mind, concluding with an invitation to the listener to join them.

Then he read a book called *Mind Games*, by Robert Masters and Jean Houston, published in 1972. Just as the Maharishi had come along at precisely the right moment in Lennon's life, echoing his point of view *plus* offering a proven method to help reach the goal he wanted to reach, Masters and Houston confirmed Lennon's own insights about psychic exploration *and* provided a structured process to help others expand their consciousness.

The authors had been involved in LSD research in the 1960s. After the government ceased to license such research, they developed alternative approaches to mind exploration based on meditation, assisted trance, and guided imagery.[1]

In *Mind Games* they set forth a series of mental adventures for small groups designed to tap into four levels of the psyche: the sensory, the psychological, the mythic, and the spiritual. They placed the "games" in the tradition of mystery schools of the distant past; seekers could find personal meaning and enlightenment in decoding the symbolic language of their own dreams and trance images and, by use of creative visualization, could improve their daily lives and stretch their own boundaries of what they thought possible.

The objective was to learn to access the unconscious mind for creative solutions to conscious problems. Not only was the unconscious mind a rich and endless resource that could be called upon whenever needed, but working within a deep trance a person could take advantage of an entirely different unreeling of time. That is, a clock in the room might register the passage of five minutes, but the perception of that elapsing time to someone who is meditating can be tremendously distorted. In five minutes of a trance state, a person might mentally rehearse an hour-long speech or go on a yearlong quest in search of the Holy Grail.

By means of the mind games in the book, participants could free themselves from negative attitudes and inhibitions and become more creative, more confident, and more mentally adventurous. In short, they could become more fully realized human beings.

The training ignited Lennon's imagination. He saw the mind games leading to a cadre of mentally liberated people infiltrated throughout a less-enlightened society—"mind guerrillas" working toward a higher purpose than their contemporaries and having a positive influence on them. To him, expanding legions of mentally liberated people would inevitably build the level of agreement necessary to bring into existence the peaceful society that was his goal.

He wrote a song of encouragement, also titled "Mind Games." Speaking in the language of dreams (clearly Lennonesque language and Lennonesque dreams), he equated the mind games process with pagan rites. In terms such as "druid dudes," "ritual dance," and "stones of your mind," he evoked the Salisbury Plain—initiates surrounded by trilithic arches, ritualized motion, earnest chanting, and communal commitment.

To those who were beginning to believe that the spirit of the sixties had died, he was advising: don't give up, keep on; keep chanting the mantra of peace and love. Let's work together as an invisible army. We'll use the power of visualization—some call it magic—to project our image of peace in space and time. We'll create an "absolute elsewhere" in our minds, an ideal so detailed and realistic that our intentions will make it manifest.

Just as athletes, speakers, entertainers—people from all walks of life—were beginning to discover the power of visualization to improve their real-life performance, Lennon suggested that peace could be manifested in the real world through the concerted efforts of individuals to visualize it.

Lennon and Ono even had a name for the absolute elsewhere, and a description. On April 1, 1973, they held a press conference to reveal them. The media assembled as requested, expecting some newsworthy comment regarding the couple's ongoing struggle to avoid deportation from the United States. Instead they listened to the following declaration: "We announce the birth of a conceptual country, NUTOPIA. Citizenship of the country can be obtained by declaration of your awareness of NUTOPIA. NUTOPIA has no land, no boundaries, no passports, only people. NUTOPIA has no laws other than cosmic. All people of NUTOPIA are ambassadors of the country. As two ambassadors of NUTOPIA, we ask for diplomatic immunity and recognition in the United Nations of our country and its people."[2]

The subtlety of the artistic concept was like enciphered text to most of those who had gathered to report the announcement, as well as to the fans who read it afterward—even when the declaration was reprinted on the album sleeve for Lennon's *Mind Games*. It seemed that almost no one comprehended the idea they were advancing. However, what had the hallmarks of a simple April Fools' Day joke on the media (and it was, on one level) actually had much deeper import.

NUTOPIA was a proposed emotional, intellectual, and spiritual union of people. It would be an imaginary union, but certainly no more imaginary than the artificial boundaries that separated people in the "real" world. According to the announcement, an individual could become a citizen of the conceptual country simply by declaring his or her awareness of it—in other words, by understanding what Lennon and Ono were trying to communicate between the lines. (Perhaps *behind the words* would be more accurate.)

"Citizens" of NUTOPIA would recognize how absurd and artificial it was to place labels on human beings: black, white, yellow, red, Japanese, British, Congolese, American, Muslim, Christian, Jew, Buddhist, conservative, liberal, socialist, capitalist, etc. Absurd because, for example, how do we categorize the offspring of a black man and a yellow woman? Or a Japanese woman who emigrates and becomes a British or American citizen? Or a Jew who converts to Christianity and later converts again to Buddhism? Is any label applied to an individual as important as his character? As important as how much personal integrity she possesses? As important as how compassionate and considerate the person is?

Citizens of NUTOPIA would mutually recognize their common humanity and their preference for peace and harmony, and they would interact in accordance with cosmic laws—*cosmic* because those are the laws that make up our innate sense of justice. To kill each other or not to kill each other? Steal from or not steal from? Respect or not respect? Cosmic laws make sense to us, as opposed to the law that we should not kill except when the act is sanctioned by the proper political or religious leader, or that we should never steal unless the legal machinery says it is permissible this time (as in, the Indians are being relocated to another region—stake out the land you want), etc.

As a citizen of NUTOPIA—that is, someone who "got it"—each individual would be an example and a proponent of the common human bond. Each would qualify to serve as an ambassador to those who had not yet gotten it.

Lennon ended the statement with his customary whimsy (much as he had ended the note returning his MBE medal with a reference to "Cold Turkey" slipping down the charts). He and Yoko asked the UN for diplomatic immunity and recognition.

The very name of their imaginary country was whimsical, as well as being cryptically self-referential for Lennon. NUTOPIA—New Utopia—was of course a modern version of the land Sir Thomas More invented in the book he published in 1516. More coined the word *Utopia* from two Greek words, *ou* (not) and *topos* (place)—that is, "no place"—or "nowhere." As a citizen of NUTOPIA, then, Lennon officially became a Nowhere Man.[3]

Those perceptive listeners who understood and embraced the absolute elsewhere of NUTOPIA would constitute the invisible army Lennon described in "Mind Games." Acting individually, but in concert, they would bring about a more harmonious world through communal visualization.

The book *Mind Games* inspired Lennon's song, but his source of inspiration for the technique of visualization was Yoko Ono. She had been telling him about it, he said, since they met.[4] The technique has an occult derivation, the idea being that on some ethereal level we are constantly in contact with the forces of the universe and that our heartfelt wishes, our prayers, communicate through the cosmos and can attract to us what we desire. A more mundane explanation is that if we focus on something we truly want, our subconscious mind will take the hint and work toward arranging it for us (i.e., if we wish passionately for riches or love or health, we will tend to motivate ourselves and be attracted to situations or behavior or opportunities that will make that outcome feasible).

Of course, the technique has its dark side. We can focus so much psychic energy on one goal—riches, for instance—that while it is becoming reality we lose our health or family. On a macro scale the implications are correspondingly greater. Wherever a society's collective imagination is focused will tend to gain power and inevitability. If that is a looming depression or foreign threat or shortage of an important resource, we can create through our words and actions the very outcome we dread.

Because Lennon believed that we all "shine on," he felt that each of us bears responsibility for part of the problem: "If you speak, what you say doesn't end here. I believe scientists could prove that vibrations go on and on infinitely, and therefore every action goes on and on infinitely and has its effect. If you carefully think out the effect you're going to create, there's more chance for all of us. It's hard to think of your every move. But your attitudes to life will have an effect on everyone—and thereby, the universe."[5]

Once, while commenting on a radio report about a demonstration against nuclear power, he provided an excellent example, on a smaller scale, of the problem of misdirected focus. Without being conscious of the fact, he said, the protesters taking part in the demonstration were calling more media attention—and thus ultimately more attention by the general public—to the very industry they opposed. They were giving it greater power. Further, regardless of how laudable their goal, everyone knew that the energy produced was essential. Therefore, their efforts were counterproductive and their positive energy squandered. Lennon argued that what they ought to be doing was devoting the same time and resources to finding and calling attention to an alternative. They ought to be focused on the solution.

The coin had two sides. Just as the collective focus could become the problem, it also presented an opportunity.

Consistent with his own insight, Lennon had already used the principle of collective visualization to plant a positive image in the public psyche. He had already written a song that offered *his* solution, *his* alternative to the nightmarish futures on which the people of his era were focused—the endless quagmire of Vietnam, world famine, Orwell's 1984, nuclear winter, apocalypse in the Middle East—as well as his prescription to end the perennial strife of our species.

He recorded and released the song in 1971; it was the one that would become his most famous anthem.

14

IMAGINE

I magine" takes on three of the most divisive issues of humankind—religion, nationalism, and possessiveness—and gently invites us to look at them from a neutral perspective.

To return for a moment to an earlier rhetorical device, let's assume our species is the subject of a study by alien visitors, a long-term anthropological study spanning thousands of earth years. The diligent aliens record in their notebooks that these featherless bipeds, while showing signs of intelligence, have remained extremely belligerent for millennia for almost unfathomable reasons. Various groups will distrust, berate, and even mercilessly slaughter members of other groups that have different belief systems—every group all the while claiming moral superiority and the partisan support of a supreme supernatural being. Individual bipeds, who have a very high statistical probability of accepting their family's belief system without ever weighing it against alternatives, will often take pride in sacrificing their own brief existence on its behalf.

In recent centuries the aliens would have observed a new type of group allegiance and belligerence. Bipeds from one region on the planet's surface will distrust, berate, and even mercilessly slaughter members of other groups because those groups live on the other side of lines that run across the natural terrain—not real lines, you understand, but imaginary lines.

They will do so even though they might share the same belief system and be physically indistinguishable from the other group of bipeds living only a short distance away. If visiting them as individuals, they would expect to exchange pleasantries, joke about their respective regions and cultural differences, and share friendship and movie recommendations. Despite this, many of the bipeds seem to take pride in sacrificing their lives or body parts on behalf of the territory bounded by imaginary lines in which they happen to have been born or simply live at the time.

Finally, the alien notebooks would bulge with examples of the bipeds' insatiable need to accumulate material items—from vehicles to sparkling stones to the latest communication devices to second and third and fourth homes—while their cousins on other continents, or perhaps only a few city blocks away, are struggling to find enough to eat.

Just how would aliens view our eccentricities? Exactly the way we would if we visited another planet and found the most intelligent species engaging in such behavior.

More than two thousand years ago, one of the more sensible bipeds reached the conclusion that "the unexamined life is not worth living." Like Socrates, Lennon prods us to examine what we generally take for granted—our religious beliefs, our nationalism, our possessive nature—then invites us to envision the improvement if we altered our point of view.

What if we accepted Lennon's assertions that neither heaven nor hell exist and that God is simply the name for a naturally occurring force in the universe—a neutral powerhouse? Without the prospect of heaven or hell, we would have no expectation of reward or punishment after death. Would we suddenly descend to barbarism, rapine, and mayhem in the streets? Possibly. More likely we would simply focus better on our existence here and now, being keenly aware of our transience and the wisdom of trying to live a full life.

What if we stopped defining ourselves by imaginary lines running across the terrain? Or at least began to think of demarcations of nations the way we think of postal districts? What if instead of considering ourselves patriots of a nation we thought of ourselves first—like the great Cynic Diogenes—as citizens of the world? Would we find it more difficult to distrust, berate, and even mercilessly slaughter fellow citizens than we would foreigners?

What if we accomplished the hardest transformation of all and overcame our possessiveness? Notice that Lennon says that imagining no heaven is "easy if you try" and imagining no countries "isn't hard to do," but as for imagining no possessions, "I wonder if you can." (For that matter, could Lennon himself have imagined moving out of his seventy-four-acre Tittenhurst estate to live in a trailer park in Muncie, donating everything he and Yoko owned to the rest of us?)

Suppose for a moment, however, that on the way to the "no possessions" state of mind we simply begin to think of our material good fortune as something to *share*? In one of their last interviews before John Lennon's death, Yoko Ono revealed that they gave 10 percent of their income to people in need.[1] How much human suffering could be alleviated if we all distributed 10 percent of our income to those less fortunate?

It is also worthwhile to note that in Lennon's mind possessions did not necessarily mean *physical* possessions. Referring to Jesus's admonition (Mark 10:25), "It is easier for a camel to go through the eye of a needle than for a rich man to enter the kingdom of God," Lennon once commented to *Playboy*: "I took it literally—that one has to dump possessions to get through to nirvana. . . . But an intellectual has less chance of getting through than me. They're possessed of ideas . . . ideas of what they're supposed to be. I'm no longer possessed of ideas."[2]

Lennon went on to clarify by observing that most people suffer under the burden of the concepts and ideas they allow to define them—ideas that are usually instilled into them by their parents and their society. The more they "own," the further they are from freedom, and the more difficult it is to squeeze through the eye of the needle and get through to the "kingdom."

The ideal world John Lennon envisaged in 1971's "Imagine" was not something he expected to see implemented in 1972. Its purpose was to serve as a possible alternative destination to the ones toward which our culture seemed to be rushing headlong in the heyday of Nixon, Brezhnev, Mao, the hot war in Southeast Asia, and the Cold War everywhere else—some version of Apocalypse 2000.

Lennon's "absolute elsewhere" represented what philosopher Richard Rorty called a "fuzzy but inspiring *focus imaginarius* . . . a handy bit of rhetoric" that might not hold up under analysis but nevertheless benefits society for having "kept the way open for political and cultural change." (Rorty claims, incidentally, that a liberal society's heroes are the poet and the revolutionary—a reasonable characterization of John Lennon, made even more apt when Rorty explains that they are "protesting in the name of the society itself against those aspects of the society which are unfaithful to its own self-image.")[3]

"Imagine" represents the distillation of Lennon's philosophy. In it he reached hardest for the universal and consciously tried to communicate a vision that would inspire everybody everywhere—from a salesclerk in Tokyo to a mechanic in Warsaw to a florist in Prague to a street musician in Barcelona to a teacher in Havana. (As proof that he did inspire them, all five cities have memorials to John Lennon.)

To the very end, he promoted the concept that all of humankind are one. Printed into the wax surrounding the label on his single "(Just Like) Starting Over"—subtle, but visible to those who took time to look—was the phrase "ONE WORLD ONE PEOPLE." Whatever distinctions people might try to impose on the world, whether racial or national, he kept arguing that they were meaningless.

Would John Lennon have altered his personal philosophy had he lived through his forties and fifties? We can only speculate. However, in his last interviews he was still talking about the importance of directing the focus of society onto solutions, rather than problems, in order to empower change. He was still comfortable with his political position in "Revolution," not supporting any wholesale change of the system unless he could first "see the plan" about what would follow. He still argued against dependence on leaders, placing emphasis on individual decision making, responsibility, and action. While acknowledging challenges in his marriage with Yoko Ono, he still saw his family life as essential to his own fulfillment as a person.

As for his secular perspective, during his July 1980 visit to Bermuda he came up with a song called "Serve Yourself." In it he offered a derisive rebuttal to Bob Dylan's recent hit "Gotta Serve Somebody," in which Dylan the evangelist tried to reduce human life to a simple dichotomy—serving God or serving Satan.

Just hours before his death, Lennon told an interviewer: "I still believe in love, peace; I still believe in positive thinking—when I can do it—I'm not *always* positive, but when I am I try and project it."

And he went on to display that perpetual open-mindedness skeptics tend to regard as gullibility, but which inoculated Lennon against becoming a dogmatic intellectual: "I'm still open to anything. I still believe almost in anything until it's disproved. I don't have any set pattern. I don't have any set answers. I'm as open as ever."[4]

Lacking any set pattern or set answers, Lennon himself never attempted to consolidate his philosophical thought in the way this book attempts to do. His personality was too now-oriented and improvisational. Up until the day he died he kept his focus on living his life, from time to time communicating his insights by posting them in the public arena in the form of songs or other creative projects. However, the structure that underpinned those occasional posted messages is discernible.

Lennon's philosophy, as noted in the introduction, was that of a man of the working class who happened to see the world through the eyes of an artist, a man of restless intelligence who was willing to question *everything* about the foundations of his life and his society. Though he was set apart from them by his great wealth and almost unprecedented fame, and though he often shocked them by actions that at first seemed offensive or at the very least controversial, millions of his fellow human beings identified with him and his search and were willing to overlook his human weaknesses and listen to what he had to say.

Why? Because with Lennon they knew they were going to hear a genuine iconoclast with the courage to speak from the heart. "I've never claimed divinity. I've never claimed purity of soul. I've never claimed to have the answer to life. I only put out songs and answer questions as honestly as I can, but *only* as honestly as I can—no more, no less."[5]

15

Shining On

A generation has passed since the death of John Lennon, an appropriate distance from which to assess him as a thinker. If the philosophical underpinnings of his creative work have gone underappreciated, it is simply because his primary medium of communication was popular music. Any radio station that might play "Mind Games" could very well broadcast, as the next song, "Boogie Oogie Oogie." Compare the lyrics of the two and it is obvious that Lennon had less in common with his contemporary songwriters than he did with the great thinkers of any age. But who pays close attention to the lyrics of popular music?

Lennon naturally derived his own insights and conclusions from his existential quest—the thinking that is explored and summarized in the preceding three chapters. But there is more to his legacy of cynical idealism than just his own conclusions. It seems fitting to end this book by calling attention to three principles growing out of his project—principles that can inspire and challenge each new generation to come:

1. We owe it to ourselves to question the "truths" our culture passes on to us and to be cynical about the motives of experts and those in authority.

2. We owe it to ourselves to live our lives as though creating works of art, using the resources fate has dealt us.

3. We owe it to ourselves and our posterity to aim at self-transformation, being aware of the "ripple" influence of our words and actions.

1. Questioning "Truths"

How many among us are truly independent thinkers? How many of us ever question the belief system of the family, community, and nation in which we grew up? What percentage of us goes from cradle to grave having lived unexamined lives?

Shouldn't we be suspicious if our thoughts and attitudes as "independent" adults habitually echo the prevailing notions of our group? Isn't it obvious that we would have different thoughts and attitudes if we were members of another culture on another continent?

Isn't it fascinating how our view of how the world works alters over time as we mature and realize how many decisions are rooted in self-interest? And isn't it mystifying that, despite that realization, we still tend to give undue weight to the opinions of authority figures and experts? Why is that? Is it because we lack confidence in the accumulated wisdom of our own experience or because we are not as liberated and independent as we would like to think we are?

In the eighteenth century—the century of the American and French Revolutions—Europe's leading thinkers began to propound the view that humankind lived in mental shackles that needed to be shaken off. These shackles, they claimed, were the product of the cultural milieu in which people were raised—the belief system and customs instilled in them by their parents, schools, and churches during their formative years.

Spearheading this movement were French intellectuals known as the *philosophes*. Montesquieu, Voltaire, Diderot, and others had responded to the reawakening of inquisitiveness that had spread through Europe with the Renaissance and the reformation of the church, and they built on the discoveries and thought of Bacon, Newton, Hobbes, Locke, and Hume.

The *philosophes* realized that the recently developed scientific method offered hope of explaining the world without resort to religious or cultural dogma, and they argued that by employing the tools of science and reason man could free himself from superstition and tradition and become the architect of his own fate. The era was labeled the Age of Reason, or the Enlightenment, and the ideas of the *philosophes* inspired Thomas Jefferson, James Madison, Benjamin Franklin, and Thomas Paine as they struggled to define and launch the new republic in America.

In Europe, Immanuel Kant expressed the hope and objective of the movement in the first paragraph of his influential essay "What is Enlightenment?" "Enlightenment is man's release from his self-incurred tutelage. Tutelage is man's inability to make use of his understanding without direction from another. Self-incurred is this tutelage when its cause lies not in lack of reason but in lack of resolution and courage to use it without direction from another. *Sapere aude!* 'Have courage to use your own reason!'—that is the motto of enlightenment."[1]

The Enlightenment may never have reached down to inspire the class of people the *philosophes* intended to reach—the person in the street—but it certainly inspired and motivated the transatlantic intelligentsia. Their response initiated what we think of as the modern era—the stretch of history marked by unprecedented advances in industry, technology, health, science, and human liberty.

Yet the overwhelming majority of people never awoke mentally to question the doctrines with which they had been inculcated—and to the doctrines of the past were added persuasive new ones such as Communism and Fascism. By the middle of the twentieth century, the torch ignited by the Enlightenment was sputtering. With scores of millions of people dead from two world wars and the Holocaust in Europe, and the most "advanced" nations of the world dreading and yet preparing for nuclear war, a reassessment began.

The tumultuous sixties offered hope. Reformers found their ranks swelled by the baby-boom children coming of age, and because so many young people were willing to challenge inherited views of the world, those views suddenly seemed quite assailable.

John Lennon matured in the midst of this new awakening. Being highly intelligent and a relentless freethinker, he managed to slip out of his own intellectual cocoon. His open-minded, heuristic approach led him to what he was convinced were valid insights, and he was more than happy to share them in interviews and through his creative projects. But like Socrates, he preferred to stimulate people to think independently. What truly mattered was that more people should wake up, look at the world through new eyes, and begin to act according to their new consciousness.

He found his own way to reach them. The Socratic method involved asking probing questions to get the target audience to think; Lennon's method used popular music as a kind of Trojan horse to implant thought-provoking lyrics into the brains of listeners.

> "God is a concept by which we measure our pain."
> "Learn how to be you in time."
> "We all shine on."

In his own populist way, Lennon restated the aims of the Enlightenment. Be an individual, he seemed to be saying. Stop accepting someone else's doctrine as your own. You are bound by mental shackles of which you are not even aware. Throw them off and define yourself.

Be critical. Question the assumptions that guide your life and remain open to new ideas—*any* new ideas. Appraise them for yourself, based on your own life experience and insights. Just always remember to be cynical about the motives of the authorities espousing the ideas you are considering. Filter out their self-interest and decide for yourself what you find valid and important.

Choose your own path. It's your right.

2. Life as a Work of Art

Assume for a moment that you discover you have some terminal condition and your doctor advises that you have only two years to live. How would you choose to spend your remaining time?

Unless you are independently wealthy, two years is too long simply to set aside your present lifestyle and live out your fantasies. You would have to accept compromises. But in any case would you choose to ignore the steadily approaching end? Would you continue to do what you do now on a daily basis? What is at stake is the dwindling remainder of your life. Wouldn't you want to indulge the passions of your heart—whatever they might be?

Perhaps you would take the trip to Tahiti or Athens or the pyramids you have always fantasized about. Perhaps you would make an effort to write the novel you've had in mind or try to leave behind a legacy of painting or sculpture or music. Perhaps you would move to the place you have yearned to live. Perhaps you would stop working such long hours and spend more time with the ones you love. Perhaps you would begin to speak up in meetings and say what you truly thought. Perhaps you would stop trying to accumulate more wealth and devote more time to philanthropic work, maybe commit yourself to work for peace or some other cause that stirs your emotions.

Perhaps you might even indulge a wild desire to try stand-up comedy, take up hang gliding, or cross the continent on a Harley-Davidson. So what if things go wrong or you fail? You will be dead anyway in two years, but you will have *lived* in the meantime.

The point is, of course, that we are all living our lives against the background ticking of a clock. Most of us have more than two years remaining; some of us have less and do not realize it.

Regardless, do any of us really want to come to the end of life without having reached out for our heart's secret passions? Which would we prefer—to look back on lives that were undirected by us, flowing along channels laid out by someone else, or lives made just as interesting and colorful and personally satisfying as we could make them by our proactive choices? Don't we owe it to ourselves to live our lives as though creating a work of art, utilizing whatever resources fate has thrown our way?

When he married Yoko Ono, John Lennon made a conscious decision to make his life his work of art. Working initially toward the goal of world peace, then branching out into the arenas of social and political justice, they staged a number of theatrical-conceptual events, all designed to focus attention on the world's inequities and point the way to something better.

Their work of art was not an elegant, finely drawn, subtly colored piece ready for display at the Salon. Far from it. What they did was improvised, controversial, and heedless of tradition. They had messy encounters with authorities, drew vitriolic attacks from critics and the public alike, and were hounded by the media; and for all their efforts they were appreciated by relatively few people. Their own marriage eventually suffered, and they separated for more than a year.

However, the experience had the strength of being authentic—they chose the path and continued to follow it because they felt it was the most valid way to spend their lives. And compare the figure of John Lennon that has come down to us as a result of his commitment to live his art with how he would be viewed today had he settled for being a wealthy ex-Beatle. Think of him living comfortably on his Tittenhurst estate and regularly churning out more Beatlesque songs for the Top Forty charts.

After 1975, when Lennon reunited with Yoko Ono, the work became more three-dimensional. He committed himself to focusing on a neglected part of his life—the domestic situation. With typical iconoclasm, he brushed aside tradition. He and Yoko redefined the gender roles within the family to suit their own dispositions.

How many philosophers take into account the domestic side of life— baking bread and tending to the needs of a growing child? For Lennon, fatherhood and the repetitive, mundane acts of family life became an enriching part of his existence, his equivalent of Gandhi's daily sessions at the spinning wheel.

In their open letter to the world published in the *New York Times* and other newspapers on May 27, 1979, Lennon and Ono very poetically described their own work-of-art-in-progress as "writing in the sky" and invited others to elevate their thinking: "Remember, we are writing in the sky instead of on paper—that's our song. Lift your eyes and look up in the sky. There's our message. Lift your eyes again and look around you, and you will see that you are walking in the sky, which extends to the ground."[2]

Grasp the poetry of the image and you will realize that, indeed, every one of us is writing a message in the sky. And if we follow Lennon's example we will not be timid about expressing ourselves on the canvas of existence. Our lives belong to us and the only thing holding us back is our own inhibitions.

In the end, our best prescription for happiness in this world is to "spend" the time fate allots to us at endeavors we enjoy and to build loving relationships.

3. Aiming at Self-Transformation

The open letter John and Yoko published in May 1979 was a quirky and often lyrical epistle that, in the midst of details about their reclusive domestic life, also offered insights into their creative thinking.

Another passage from that letter described a technique they used to respond to a person who was angry with them—by mentally drawing a halo around his or her head. The point was not whether the person stopped being angry but the shift in their own consciousness. As a consequence of the mental trick, they stopped seeing him or her as an angry person and instead saw an angel.[3]

When compared with recommendations that the one sure way to bring about peace in Iraq is for the Marines to annihilate every resister, the sentiment the two were expressing seems hopelessly naive and irrelevant to the world's problems.

Is it? Well, have thousands of years of annihilating the "enemy" brought peace to the world? When anger is met with anger, is a peaceful resolution on the way?

What underlies the suggestion to draw a mental halo around the person who is angry at us is a radical shift in perspective. Call it detachment. Call it spirituality. Call it uncommon sense. Nothing in our relationship with the person will necessarily be changed—he or she may very well remain angry—but at least we will not escalate the confrontation. Since most people are not naturally malicious, what results is an opportunity to reduce and maybe neutralize the bad feelings.

But in order to resist the natural inclination to respond in kind, our perspective must be shifted. To learn to see in a new way we need to transform ourselves.

Nothing *requires* us to do so. We can choose to go through our entire lives seeing the world as a shark tank, where the shrewdest course is to take care of Number One and the person who dies with the most toys wins. Pick your cliché. However, we need to realize that it is a *choice* we are making. We all know that the world isn't really a shark tank (with the possible exception of a few circles in Washington and Hollywood). It's just that people tend to get caught up in their daily struggles and start to act and react impulsively. They have heightened motivations and human shortcomings.

As readily as we can choose to see the world as dog-eat-dog, we can choose to see it as a budding utopia. How we see it influences how we act. How we act influences those around us. Thus, every day we are faced with a simple choice: contribute to the creation of a world we find repugnant or contribute to the creation of a world we find satisfying.

Does this sound like the airheaded reasoning of a rock star?

Then consider the example of one simple choice by one seemingly insignificant person. On December 1, 1955, Rosa Parks took a seat on a bus in Montgomery, Alabama, after a hard day of work as a seamstress in a department store. Before long she was asked to give up her seat to a white man. The law was on his side. According to the city's transportation rules at that time, she was required, as a person of color, either to move to the back of the bus or to ride standing while the white man sat. However, Rosa Parks believed that the rule was unjust, and she was tired of giving in to discrimination, so she continued to sit there until finally the police were summoned and she was led away under arrest.

Her case was championed by local civic groups and African-American churches. They organized a boycott of city buses, insisting on equal rights and courtesy for all Montgomery citizens and the hiring of black drivers. The boycott would continue for more than a year. Transit revenues dropped. Passions were inflamed. On January 30, 1956, the house of the movement's leader, Dr. Martin Luther King, Jr., was destroyed by a bomb. The boycotters persisted regardless and the legal wrangling ultimately went to the United States Supreme Court.

In December 1956, the highest court in the land declared the rules unconstitutional, and as a result black residents of Montgomery were no longer allowed to be treated like second-class citizens on public transportation. Further, other people were inspired by the example of Rosa Parks to take stands of their own. The Civil Rights Movement got underway, and a century of state-sanctioned discrimination crumbled before the forces unleashed.

All from the act of one individual faced with a simple choice.

Perhaps none of the choices we make will ever have the far-reaching consequences of the one made by Rosa Parks, but who knows? At the time she made it, could she have imagined how far out the ripples would extend?

Martin Luther King's conduct is also instructive. Had he responded to the anger of the white community with anger, had he responded to the bombing of his house by condoning reciprocal attacks, the violence would have been perpetuated. Instead, working from a model developed by Mahatma Gandhi, he urged restraint. He understood that the intolerance and hatred he faced were founded on ignorance, and he believed that most members of the white community confronting him actually had good hearts.

When John Lennon argued that people have the power to reshape society if they will only recognize that power, he was simply expressing the obvious—the obvious truth that people for some reason find very difficult to believe, no matter how many examples like that of Rosa Parks are placed in front of them.

Yet it is vitally important that we do believe and make the effort to transform ourselves, not just for our own society but for posterity. As Lennon remarked elsewhere in the open letter—in a profound insight masked in another expression of the obvious: "The future of the earth is up to all of us."[4]

Suggested Listening
"Instant Karma (We All Shine On)"
"Mind Games"
"Imagine"

EPILOGUE

When John Lennon ended his respite from public life midway through 1980, he was bursting with creativity and new musical ideas. The time had come to "breathe out."

John and Yoko, in the prime of life, thought it reasonable that they might live for another forty years. Rich, accomplished, and world-famous, they were fully aware of their tremendous potential to help shape the world in a positive way.

They toyed with ideas for how best to allocate their remaining four decades. First on the list was to record the new music they had both been accumulating. They found a producer, chose backup musicians, and booked a series of recording sessions to put the new songs on tape. *Double Fantasy* resulted, an album featuring songs from both of them on alternating tracks.

But there was still more material, and the creative juices were flowing. They returned to the studio. On the night of December 8, 1980, they returned home after working on Yoko's song, "Walking on Thin Ice." John declined a suggestion to stop somewhere for dinner; he had a desire to see his son before the five-year-old went to bed for the night.

Near the entrance to the Dakota apartment building lurked a man with a pistol. He was a man of the sort the Enlightenment *philosophes* knew all too well—a man so mired in ignorance that he was blind to the potential he was bringing to an end.

We will never know what John Lennon might have accomplished given a few more decades. What we do know is that he was a superstar who still shines on.

Not in the way that a celebrity such as Elvis Presley does—although his music still stirs every new generation that discovers him. Lennon shines on as a beacon of peace and truth. More than a beacon, he remains a dynamo with the power to inspire—especially when the darkness comes closing in.

Eleven years after his death, when armed forces began to assemble across the Mideast for the Gulf War of 1991, Yoko marshaled the forces of peace in response. She proposed an updating of "Give Peace a Chance," and some forty stars hurried to join her and Sean as members of The Peace Choir—among them Peter Gabriel, Tom Petty, Bonnie Raitt, Little Richard, and Lenny Kravitz.

In the aftermath of 9/11, "Imagine" was suppressed from airplay by authorities who, presumably, believed that its call to "imagine there's no heaven" might offend raw sensibilities. In the all-star telethon held ten days later, *America: A Tribute to Heroes*, Neil Young deliberately chose it to perform. What better way to repudiate the religious extremism behind the heinous attack than Lennon's gentle anthem?

And what better song to reflect the unifying spirit of the Olympic Games? Following introductory comments by Yoko, Peter Gabriel performed "Imagine" for the opening ceremony of the 2006 Winter Olympic Games in Turin, Italy.

More recently, Lennon's iconic status was evoked to focus attention on and help end the suffering in the Darfur region of Sudan. In July 2007, Yoko authorized the release of *Instant Karma: The Amnesty International Campaign to Save Darfur*. Luminaries from the world of music, including U2, Green Day, Willie Nelson, Aerosmith, and Christina Aguilera, covered classic Lennon songs. All profits went to relief for the stricken region.

Like "the moon and the stars and the sun," John Lennon still shines on. Let us bear in mind that—as he assured us in a song—so do we all.

CHRONOLOGY

1940:   John Winston Lennon born in Liverpool on October 9.

1946:   Moves in with his Aunt Mary Elizabeth ("Mimi") and her husband George Smith. Final abandonment by his father, Alfred Lennon, in July.

1952:   Begins classes at Quarry Bank High School in September.

1955:   In June loses his uncle and substitute father George Smith, who dies suddenly of a hemorrhaged liver.

1956:   Discovers rock 'n' roll and Elvis Presley via Radio Luxembourg.

1957:   Forms a skiffle group, the Quarrymen, in March. The band gives its first performance on June 9 at Liverpool's Empire Theatre. Meets Paul McCartney at a performance on July 6. Enters Liverpool College of Art in September, where he meets his future wife Cynthia Powell and his closest friend, Stuart Sutcliffe.

1958:   George Harrison joins the Quarrymen in February. Julia, Lennon's mother, dies in an accident on July 15.

1960:   In May, Lennon's group, now known as the Silver Beetles, is booked on its first tour as backup band for Johnny Gentle. Lennon leaves Liverpool College of Art in July. On August 16, the Beatles depart England for a booking at the Indra Club in Hamburg, Germany.

1961: First performance at the Cavern in March. Brian Epstein visits the Cavern on November 9. Epstein offers to manage the group on December 3.

1962: Lennon marries pregnant Cynthia Powell in August. "Love Me Do" released in October.

1963: "Please Please Me" hits number one on March 2. Son John Charles Julian born on April 8. Beatlemania strikes in November.

1964: The Beatles first appear on *Ed Sullivan Show* on February 9. *In His Own Write* published in March. *A Hard Day's Night* premieres in July.

1965: *A Spaniard in the Works* published in June. *Help!* premieres in July. In October, Queen Elizabeth II names Lennon a Member of the Order of the British Empire.

1966: Some time during the winter, Lennon reads *The Passover Plot* and *The Psychedelic Experience*. In a March interview, he asserts that the Beatles are more popular than Jesus. In April, he records "Tomorrow Never Knows," his first LSD-inspired song. The U.S. magazine *Datebook* reprints Lennon's Jesus-related comments in late July. Over thirty-five radio stations ban Beatles music, and across the Bible Belt their records are tossed into bonfires. Lennon apologizes on August 12. In September, he begins filming *How I Won the War*. He meets Yoko Ono at the Indica Gallery on November 9.

1967: *Sgt. Pepper's Lonely Hearts Club Band* released on June 1. "All You Need Is Love" debuts live worldwide on June 25. Lennon meets the Maharishi Mahesh Yogi on August 24.

1968: In February, he flies to northern India for a spiritual retreat at the Maharishi's center in Rishikesh. The visit is cut short in April over allegations about the Maharishi's interactions with women. In May, Lennon invites Yoko Ono to his Weybridge home. In June, they plant acorns together at Coventry Cathedral. Lennon's first art exhibition, You Are Here, opens July 1. Police discover cannabis resin in his flat on October 18. On November 8, Cynthia officially divorces him. Controversial *Two Virgins* album released November 29.

1969: Lennon marries Yoko Ono in Gibraltar on March 20. Amsterdam bed-in for peace takes place March 25–31. In late May a second bed-in begins in Montreal, during which Lennon writes and records "Give Peace a Chance." Lennon returns his MBE to the queen in November. "WAR IS OVER!" billboards go up for Christmas. On December 23, Lennon and Ono confer with Canadian Prime Minister Pierre Trudeau about the peace movement. On December 30, British company ATV produces an hour-long special naming Lennon—along with John F. Kennedy and Ho Chi Minh—as "Man of the Decade."

1970: Bag One, the Erotic Lithographs exhibit, debuts in the London Arts Gallery in January. Lennon writes and records "Instant Karma" on January 27. On April 10, Paul McCartney officially leaves the Beatles. In late April, Lennon and Ono visit Los Angeles to undergo Primal Scream therapy under Arthur Janov. *Plastic Ono Band* album released in December, a statement of philosophy that includes "Working Class Hero," "God," and "I Found Out."

1971: In September, Lennon and Ono leave England for New York City, a visit that will become permanent. *Imagine* album released in October. Lennon and Ono appear at the John Sinclair rally in December, unaware of FBI informants in the audience.

1972: In March, Lennon and Ono are served with deportation orders, initiating a four-year fight to remain in the U.S. In May, Lennon announces on national television that his telephone is being tapped. *Some Time in New York City* is released in June.

1973: Lennon and Ono separate in October, beginning his "lost weekend." *Mind Games* album released in November.

1974: In March, Lennon is ejected from Troubadour nightclub in Los Angeles, symptomatic of his unstable behavior without Ono. *Walls and Bridges* released in October. "Whatever Gets You thru the Night" becomes the number one U.S. single on November 16. Lennon fulfills a promise to Elton John on November 28, performing at John's Madison Square Garden concert.

1975: Lennon moves back in with Yoko Ono in January. On October 7, the New York State Supreme Court reverses the deportation order, requiring that Lennon's request for resident status be reconsidered. On October 9, Yoko Ono gives birth to their only child together, a boy they name Sean Taro Ono Lennon.

1976: Lennon's contract with EMI/Capitol expires in February, freeing him from all creative commitments. In July, his legal battle to remain in the United States ends when his application to become a permanent resident is granted at a special hearing.

1979: On May 27, responding to ongoing curiosity about their hiatus from public life, Lennon and Ono place a full-page ad in several prominent world newspapers, "A Love Letter from John and Yoko. To People Who Ask Us What, When and Why."

1980: Lennon charters a small schooner in July and sails from Rhode Island to Bermuda. While on the island he writes songs for *Double Fantasy*, his joint album with Ono. In September, Lennon and Ono reemerge into the public eye, beginning with an exhaustive interview with *Playboy* magazine. On December 8, 10:50 p.m., one more icon of peace falls to gunfire.

Notes

Introduction

1. David Sheff, *All We Are Saying* (New York: St Martin's, Griffin, 2000), 193. From the Playboy Interview: John Lennon and Yoko Ono, *Playboy* Magazine (January 1981). © 1980 by Playboy.

2. William J. Dowlding, *Beatlesongs* (New York: Simon and Schuster, Fireside, 1989), 117.

3. Pete Shotton and Nicholas Schaffner, *John Lennon in My Life* (Briarcliff Manor, NY: Stein and Day, 1983), 117.

4. Ibid.

5. Ibid.

6. Jann S. Wenner, *Lennon Remembers* (New York: Verso, 2000), 136–37; Vic Garbarini and Brian Cullman, with Barbara Graustark, *Strawberry Fields Forever: John Lennon Remembered* (New York: Bantam, Delilah, 1980), 113.

7. Jonathan Cott and Christine Doudna, eds., *The Ballad of John and Yoko* (Garden City, NY: Doubleday, 1982), 280.

Chapter One

1. Philip Norman, *Shout! The Beatles in Their Generation* (New York: Simon and Shuster, Fireside, 1981), 55–56.

2. Bill Harry, *The John Lennon Encyclopedia* (London: Virgin Publishing, 2000), 477.

3. Julia Baird, *John Lennon, My Brother* (New York: Henry Holt, 1988), 9.

4. Harry, *John Lennon Encyclopedia*, 478–81.

5. Ibid.

6. Ibid., 512.

7. Baird, *John Lennon, My Brother*, 11.

8. Ibid., 12–13.

9. Ray Coleman, *Lennon* (New York: McGraw-Hill, 1985), 21–22.

10. Baird, *John Lennon, My Brother*, 13–14.

11. Coleman, *Lennon*, 31.

12. Ibid.

Chapter Two

1. Coleman, *Lennon*, 25 (see chap. 1, n. 9).

2. *Funk & Wagnalls New Encyclopedia* (New York: Rand McNally and Company, 1986), s.v. "Great Britain," 12:149.

3. Ibid.

4. Shotton and Schaffner, *John Lennon in My Life*, 31 (see intro., n. 3).

5. Coleman, *Lennon*, 30–31.

6. Shotton and Schaffner, *John Lennon in My Life*, 38.

7. Coleman, *Lennon*, 26, 38; Baird, *John Lennon, My Brother*, 33 (see chap. 1, n. 3); Shotton and Schaffner, *John Lennon in My Life*, 33.

8. Wenner, *Lennon Remembers*, 36 (see intro., n. 6).

9. Shotton and Schaffner, *John Lennon in My Life*, 31–32.

10. Ibid., 32.

11. Ibid., 33–34.

12. Coleman, *Lennon*, 3.

13. Ibid., 158–9.

14. Ibid., 2.

15. Ibid., 54.

16. Coleman, *Lennon*, 63; Jim O'Donnell, *The Day John Met Paul* (New York: Penguin, 1996), 46, 76; Shotton and Schaffner, *John Lennon in My Life*, 52.

17. O'Donnell, *Day John Met Paul*, 46.

18. Ibid., 113–21.

19. Coleman, *Lennon*, 73, 108, 598.

Chapter Three

1. Norman, *Shout!* 64–65 (see chap. 1, n. 1); Coleman, *Lennon*, 111 (see chap. 1, n. 9).

2. Coleman, *Lennon*, 112.

3. Ibid., 113, 115–6.

4. Ibid., 118; Pete Best and Patrick Doncaster, *Beatle! The Pete Best Story* (New York: Dell Publishing Co., Inc., 1985), 49.

5. Coleman, *Lennon*, 119.

6. Best and Doncaster, *Pete Best Story*, 46.

7. Coleman, *Lennon*, 130.

8. Harry, *John Lennon Encyclopedia*, 456 (see chap. 1, n. 2).

9. Coleman, *Lennon*, 120–30.

10. Cynthia Lennon, *A Twist of Lennon* (New York: Avon Books, 1980), 54.

11. Best and Doncaster, *Pete Best Story*, 71–76.

12. Ibid., 81–82.

13. Norman, *Shout!* 110–11.

14. Coleman, *Lennon*, 599, 601.

15. Best and Doncaster, *Pete Best Story*, 104–7, 126; Norman, *Shout!* 134.

16. Brian Epstein, *A Cellarful of Noise* (New York: Pocket Books, 1998), 94–100.

17. Ibid., 108.

18. Dowlding, *Beatlesongs*, 30 (see intro., n. 2).

19. Ibid., 29.

20. Harry, *John Lennon Encyclopedia*, 720–21.

21. Norman, *Shout!* 170.

22. Peter Brown and Steven Gaines, *The Love You Make* (New York: Signet, 1984), 84.

23. Harry, *John Lennon Encyclopedia*, 218.

24. Wenner, *Lennon Remembers*, 148 (see intro., n. 6).

25. Harry, *John Lennon Encyclopedia*, 311.

26. Coleman, *Lennon*, 223.

27. Shotton and Schaffner, *John Lennon in My Life*, 117 (see intro., n. 3).

28. Ibid., 110.

29. Sheff, *All We Are Saying*, 196. From the Playboy Interview: John Lennon and Yoko Ono, *Playboy* Magazine (January 1981). © 1980 by Playboy.

Chapter Four

1. Viktor E. Frankl, *Man's Search for Meaning* (New York: Washington Square, 1985), 128.

2. Ibid., 128, 132.

3. Hugh Schonfield, *The Passover Plot* (Rockport, MA: Element, 1993), 119.

4. Zechariah 9:9. Translation by Hugh Schonfield.

5. John Robertson, *The Art & Music of John Lennon* (London: Omnibus Press, 1990), 199; Coleman, *Lennon*, 312 (see chap. 1, n. 9).

6. Steve Turner, *The Gospel According to the Beatles* (Louisville: Westminster John Knox Press, 2006), 22–25.

7. Coleman, *Lennon*, 315.

8. Ibid., 316.

9. Brown and Gaines, *Love You Make*, 194 (see chap. 3, n. 22).

10. Sheff, *All We Are Saying*, 127. From the Playboy Interview: John Lennon and Yoko Ono, *Playboy* Magazine (January 1981). © 1980 by Playboy.

11. Coleman, *Lennon*, 438.

12. Cott and Doudna, *Ballad of John and Yoko*, 68 (see intro., n. 7).

13. Garbarini and Cullman, *Strawberry Fields Forever*, 103 (see intro., n. 6).

14. Ibid.

15. Harry, *John Lennon Encyclopedia*, 8–9 (see chap. 1, n. 2).

16. James Sauceda, *The Literary Lennon* (Ann Arbor, MI: The Pierian Press, 1983), 103–4.

Chapter Five

1. Turner, *Gospel According to the Beatles*, 115–16 (see chap. 4, n. 6); Brown and Gaines, *Love You Make*, 157–59 (see chap. 3, n. 22).

2. Turner, *Gospel According to the Beatles*, 19.

3. Lennon, *Twist of Lennon*, 155 (see chap. 3, n. 10).

4. Shotton and Schaffner, *John Lennon in My Life*, 118 (see intro., n. 3).

5. Wenner, *Lennon Remembers*, 52 (see intro., n. 6).

6. Shotton and Schaffner, *John Lennon in My Life*, 133.

7. Harry, *John Lennon Encyclopedia*, 135–36 (see chap. 1, n. 2).

8. Coleman, *Lennon*, 444 (see chap. 1, n. 9).

9. Wenner, *Lennon Remembers*, 106–7.

Chapter Six

1. Dowlding, *Beatlesongs*, 96 (see intro., n. 2).

2. Brown & Gaines, *Love You Make*, 201 (see chap. 3, n. 22).

3. Paul Mason, *The Maharishi* (Rockport, MA: Element Books, 1994), 105.

4. Shotton and Schaffner, *John Lennon in My Life*, 137 (see intro., n. 3).

5. Mason, *Maharishi*, 108.

6. Brown & Gaines, *Love You Make*, 240–41.

7. Mason, *Maharishi*, 106–7.

8. Brown & Gaines, *Love You Make*, 242–43.

9. Cynthia Lennon, *Twist of Lennon*, 164 (see chap. 3, n. 10).

10. Shotton and Schaffner, *John Lennon in My Life*, 143.

11. Mason, *Maharishi*, 181.

12. Coleman, *Lennon*, 340 (see chap. 1, n. 9).

13. Mason, *Maharishi*, 50.

14. Shotton and Schaffner, *John Lennon in My Life*, 139.

15. Mason, *Maharishi*, 132.

16. Ibid., 74–75, 96–97.

17. Harold H. Bloomfield, M.D., Michael Peter Cain, and Dennis T. Jaffe, *TM*: Discovering Inner Energy and Overcoming Stress* (New York: Delacorte Press, 1975), 183–84.

18. Ibid., 184.

19. Mason, *Maharishi*, 134.

20. Norman, *Shout!*, 323 (see chap. 1, n. 1).

21. Ibid.

22. Brown & Gaines, *Love You Make*, 261.

23. Wenner, *Lennon Remembers*, 27–28 (see intro., n. 6).

24. Mason, *Maharishi*, 257.

25. Mia Farrow, *What Falls Away* (New York: Doubleday, Nan A. Talese, 1997), 140–41.

26. Jon Wiener, *Come Together: John Lennon in His Time* (Urbana and Chicago: Illini Books, 1991), 177.

27. John Lennon, *Skywriting by Word of Mouth* (New York: Harper & Row, 1986), 33–34.

Chapter Seven

1. Luis E. Navia, *Diogenes of Sinope: The Man in the Tub* (Westport, CT: Greenwood, 1998), 158, 165. Diogenes apparently coined the word *cosmopolitan* ("a citizen of the cosmos") on the spot. See page 23.

2. Ibid., 21. The disrespect was mutual. Plato called Diogenes "a Socrates gone mad."

3. Ibid., 2–3.

4. Ibid., 158. Apparently not amused, and completely ignoring (or missing) the point, Plato responded by amending the definition: "having broad nails."

5. Ibid., 160, 164.

6. Baird, *John Lennon, My Brother*, 79 (see chap. 1, n. 3).

7. Shotton and Schaffner, *John Lennon in My Life*, 103 (see intro., n. 3); Baird, *John Lennon, My Brother*, 81–82.

8. Shotton and Schaffner, *John Lennon in My Life*, 148–60.

9. Wenner, *Lennon Remembers*, 28 (see intro., n. 6).

10. Garbarini and Cullman, *Strawberry Fields Forever*, 101 (see intro., n. 6).

11. Wenner, *Lennon Remembers*, 45.

12. Sheff, *All We Are Saying*, 202 (see intro., n. 1); Shotton and Schaffner, *John Lennon in My Life*, 179.

13. Wenner, *Lennon Remembers*, 128–30.

14. Ibid., 33–34; Norman, *Shout!* 362–70 (see chap. 1, n.1).

15. Brown & Gaines, *Love You Make*, 329 (see chap. 3, n. 22).

16. Sheff, *All We Are Saying*, 123. From the Playboy Interview: John Lennon and Yoko Ono, *Playboy* Magazine (January 1981). © 1980 by Playboy.

17. Ibid., 125, 128.

18. Ibid.

19. Coleman, *Lennon*, 316 (see chap. 1, n. 9).

20. Ibid., 320.

21. David Wallechinsky and Irving Wallace, *The People's Almanac* (Garden City, NY: Doubleday, 1975), 253.

22. Sheff, *All We Are Saying*, 187. From the Playboy Interview: John Lennon and Yoko Ono, *Playboy* Magazine (January 1981). © 1980 by Playboy.

Chapter Eight

1. Sheff, *All We Are Saying*, 102–4. From the Playboy Interview: John Lennon and Yoko Ono, *Playboy* Magazine (January 1981). © 1980 by Playboy.

2. Harry, *John Lennon Encyclopedia*, 683 (see chap. 1, n. 2); Shotton and Schaffner, *John Lennon in My Life*, 138 (see intro., n. 3).

3. Norman, *Shout!* 331 (see chap. 1, n. 1).

4. Coleman, *Lennon*, 341 (see chap. 1, n. 9).

5. Norman, *Shout!* 332; Harry, *John Lennon Encyclopedia*, 683; Wenner, *Lennon Remembers*, 40 (see intro., n. 6).

6. Shotton and Schaffner, *John Lennon in My Life*, 168–69.

7. Garbarini and Cullman, *Strawberry Fields Forever*, 101 (see intro., n. 6).

8. Brown & Gaines, *Love You Make*, 3, 7, 273 (see chap. 3, n. 22).

9. Anthony Fawcett, *John Lennon: One Day at a Time* (New York: Grove, 1981), 18.

10. Ibid., 21.

11. Ibid., 21–24.

12. Ibid., 34–38.

13. Ibid., 38.

14. Coleman, *Lennon*, 606–7. (And subsequent dates in series.)

15. Harry, *John Lennon Encyclopedia*, 712–13.

16. Fawcett, *One Day*, 41.

17. Ibid., 40.

18. Cott and Doudna, *Ballad of John and Yoko*, 171 (see intro., n. 7).

19. Robertson, *Art & Music*, 95, 131, 134 (see chap. 4, n. 5).

20. Fawcett, *One Day*, 171–73.

21. Cott and Doudna, *Ballad of John and Yoko*, 66.

Chapter Nine

1. Wiener, *Come Together*, 88 (see chap. 6, n. 26).

2. Sheff, *All We Are Saying*, 108. From the Playboy Interview: John Lennon and Yoko Ono, *Playboy* Magazine (January 1981). © 1980 by Playboy.

3. Fawcett, *One Day*, 49 (see chap. 8, n. 9); Cott and Doudna, *Ballad of John and Yoko*, xxi (see intro., n. 7); Wiener, *Come Together*, 89.

4. Fawcett, *One Day*, 49.

5. Schonfield, *Passover Plot*, 187 (see chap. 4, n. 3).

6. Fawcett, *One Day*, 54.

7. Ibid., 51.

8. Harry, *John Lennon Encyclopedia*, 4 (see chap. 1, n. 2).

9. Wiener, *Come Together*, 92.

10. Ibid., 93.

11. Shotton and Schaffner, *John Lennon in My Life*, 192 (see intro., n. 3).

12. Harry, *John Lennon Encyclopedia*, 276.

13. Ibid., 276–77.

14. Ibid., 277–78.

15. Paul Du Noyer, *We All Shine On* (New York: HarperCollins, 1997), 26.

16. Brown & Gaines, *Love You Make*, 167 (see chap. 3, n. 22).

17. Fawcett, *One Day*, 57; Brown & Gaines, *Love You Make*, 330.

18. Fawcett, *One Day*, 58.

19. Ibid., 57.

20. Ibid., 58.

21. Ibid., 59.

22. Ibid., 65–67.

Chapter Ten

1. Wiener, *Come Together*, 110–13 (see chap. 6, n. 26).

2. Coleman, *Lennon*, 611 (see chap. 1, n. 9); Wiener, *Come Together*, 110; Harry, *John Lennon Encyclopedia*, 306 (see chap. 1, n. 2).

3. BBC News, "Hanratty: The Damning DNA," May 10, 2002, http://news.bbc.co.uk/2/hi/uk_news/wales/1980731.stm.

4. Wiener, *Come Together*, 115–16.

5. Coleman, *Lennon*, 613; Brown & Gaines, *Love You Make*, 334 (see chap. 3, n. 22).

6. Wiener, *Come Together*, 118–23.

7. Coleman, *Lennon*, 613.

8. Barbara Graustark, "The Real John Lennon," *Newsweek*, September 29, 1980, 76.

9. Wiener, *Come Together*, 159.

10. Ibid., 167–68.

11. Ibid., 154; John Lennon, *Skywriting*, 25 (see chap. 6, n. 27).

12. Fawcett, *One Day*, 121–23 (see chap. 8, n. 9).

13. Wiener, *Come Together*, 174–75.

14. Harry, *John Lennon Encyclopedia*, 812–13.

15. Wiener, *Come Together*, 197.

16. Ibid., 200.

17. Ibid., 208.

18. Ibid., 183.

19. Brown & Gaines, *Love You Make*, 11, 330.

20. Sheff, *All We Are Saying*, 182. From the Playboy Interview: John Lennon and Yoko Ono, *Playboy* Magazine (January 1981). © 1980 by Playboy.

21. Wiener, *Come Together*, 213–15.

22. Du Noyer, *We All Shine On*, 64 (see chap. 9, n. 15).

23. Jon Wiener, *Gimme Some Truth* (Berkeley and Los Angeles: University of California Press, 1999), 113.

24. Ibid., 138–39.

25. Wiener, *Come Together*, 225.

26. Ibid., 229.

27. Sheff, *All We Are Saying*, 115. From the Playboy Interview: John Lennon and Yoko Ono, *Playboy* Magazine (January 1981). © 1980 by Playboy.

28. Wiener, *Gimme Some Truth*, 88, 179, 253.

29. Ibid., 2.

30. Ibid., 114–15, 250–51.

31. Ibid., 56–57, 236.

32. Wiener, *Come Together*, 271, 278–79, 294–95.

33. Ibid., 253.

34. John Lennon, *Skywriting*, 23.

35. Wiener, *Come Together*, 267.

36. Harry, *John Lennon Encyclopedia*, 635.

37. Wiener, *Come Together*, 273.

38. Du Noyer, *We All Shine On*, 84.

39. Cott and Doudna, *Ballad of John and Yoko*, 150 (see intro., n. 7).

Chapter Eleven

1. Sheff, *All We Are Saying*, 13. From the Playboy Interview: John Lennon and Yoko Ono, *Playboy* Magazine (January 1981). © 1980 by Playboy.

2. Garbarini and Cullman, *Strawberry Fields Forever*, 102 (see intro., n. 6).

3. Jonathan Cott, "John Lennon," *Playboy* interview, January 22, 1981.

4. Cott and Doudna, *Ballad of John and Yoko*, 167 (see intro., n. 7); British Broadcasting Corporation, *The Lennon Tapes* (London: BBC Publications, 1991), 75.

5. Garbarini and Cullman, *Strawberry Fields Forever*, 118.

6. Sheff, *All We Are Saying*, 15. From the Playboy Interview: John Lennon and Yoko Ono, *Playboy* Magazine (January 1981). © 1980 by Playboy.

7. Ibid.

8. Cott and Doudna, *Ballad of John and Yoko*, 168–69.

9. Wiener, *Come Together*, 288 (see chap. 6, n. 26); Harry, *John Lennon Encyclopedia*, 54 (see chap. 1, n. 2).

10. Garbarini and Cullman, *Strawberry Fields Forever*, 175.

11. Sheff, *All We Are Saying*, 46. From the Playboy Interview: John Lennon and Yoko Ono, *Playboy* Magazine (January 1981). © 1980 by Playboy.

12. Ibid., 78.

13. Anthony Elliot, *The Mourning of John Lennon* (Berkeley: University of California Press, 1999), 134–35.

14. Cott, *Playboy* interview.

Chapter Twelve

1. Wenner, *Lennon Remembers*, 136–37 (see intro., n. 6).

2. Garbarini and Cullman, *Strawberry Fields Forever*, 113 (see intro., n. 6).

3. Leonard Gross, "John Lennon: A Shorn Beatle Tries It on His Own," *Look*, December 13, 1966.

4. Wiener, *Come Together*, 276–77 (see chap. 6, n. 26).

5. Michel W. Potts, "Arun Gandhi Shares the Mahatma's Message," *India–West* 27, no. 13 (February 2002), A34.

6. Joel Stein, "Just Say Om," *Time*, August 4, 2003, 51–53, 55.

7. Cott, *Playboy* interview.

8. Sheff, *All We Are Saying*, 120. From the Playboy Interview: John Lennon and Yoko Ono, *Playboy* Magazine (January 1981). © 1980 by Playboy.

9. Geoffrey Giuliano and Brenda Giuliano, *The Lost Lennon Interviews* (Holbrook, MA: Adams Corporation, 1996), 56.

10. Sheff, *All We Are Saying*, 131. From the Playboy Interview: John Lennon and Yoko Ono, *Playboy* Magazine (January 1981). © 1980 by Playboy.

11. Giuliano and Giuliano, *Lost Lennon Interviews*, 93.

12. Sheff, *All We Are Saying*, 126. From the Playboy Interview: John Lennon and Yoko Ono, *Playboy* Magazine (January 1981). © 1980 by Playboy.

13. Harry, *John Lennon Encyclopedia*, 400–1 (see chap. 1, n. 2).

Chapter Thirteen

1. Robert Masters and Jean Houston, *Mind Games: The Guide to Inner Space* (Wheaton, IL: Quest Books, 1998), xi.

2. Du Noyer, *We All Shine On*, 75 (see chap. 9, n. 15).

3. Ibid., 76.

4. Sheff, *All We Are Saying*, 38 (see intro., n. 1).

5. Giuliano and Giuliano, *Lost Lennon Interviews*, 52 (see chap. 12, n. 9).

Chapter Fourteen

1. Sheff, *All We Are Saying*, 97 (see intro., n. 1).

2. Ibid., 99.

3. Richard Rorty, *Contingency, Irony, and Solidarity* (New York: Cambridge University Press, 1989), 60, 195.

4. Bob Miles, *Testimony: The Life and Times of John Lennon in His Own Words* (Buckinghamshire, U.K.: Magnum Music Group, 1995), track 7, track 11.

5. Cott and Doudna, *Ballad of John and Yoko*, 190 (see intro., n. 7).

Chapter Fifteen

1. Immanuel Kant, "What is Enlightenment?" in *Foundations of the Metaphysics of Morals* (Indianapolis: The Liberal Arts Press, Inc., 1959), 85.

2. Garbarini and Cullman, *Strawberry Fields Forever*, 176 (see intro., n. 6).

3. Ibid., 175.

4. Ibid.

Bibliography

Aldridge, Alan, ed. *The Beatles Illustrated Lyrics.* New York: Black Dog and Leventhal, 1999.

Baird, Julia. *John Lennon, My Brother.* New York: Henry Holt, 1988.

Bartley, William Warren, III. *Wittgenstein.* LaSalle, IL: Open Court, 1988.

Beatles, The. *The Beatles Lyrics.* Compilation. London: Futura, 1983.

Best, Pete, and Patrick Doncaster. *Beatle! The Pete Best Story.* New York: Dell, 1985.

Bhaktivedanta Book Trust. *Search for Liberation.* Los Angeles: Bhaktivedanta Book Trust, 1981. (Featuring a conversation between A. C. Bhaktivedanta, Swami Prabhupada, and John Lennon.)

Bloomfield, Harold H., M.D., Michael Peter Cain, Dennis T. Jaffe. *TM*: Discovering Inner Energy and Overcoming Stress.* New York: Delacorte, 1975.

Borradori, Giovanna. *The American Philosopher.* Chicago: University of Chicago Press, 1994.

British Broadcasting Corporation. *The Lennon Tapes.* (John Lennon and Yoko Ono in Conversation with Andy Peebles, 6 December 1980). London: BBC Publications, 1981.

Brown, Peter, and Steven Gaines. *The Love You Make.* New York: Signet, 1984.

Canadian Broadcasting Company. *John & Yoko's Year of Peace.* DVD. Chatsworth, CA: CBC Home Video, 2000.

Coleman, Ray. *Lennon.* New York: McGraw-Hill, 1985.

Cooper, Lane, trans. *Plato on the Trial and Death of Socrates.* Ithaca, NY: Cornell University Press, 1974.

Cott, Jonathan. "John Lennon." *Playboy*, January 22, 1981.

Cott, Jonathan, and Christine Doudna, eds. *The Ballad of John and Yoko.* Garden City, NY: Doubleday, 1982.

Dowlding, William J. *Beatlesongs.* New York: Simon and Schuster, Fireside, 1989.

Du Noyer, Paul. *We All Shine On.* New York: HarperCollins, 1997.

Durant, Will. *The Story of Philosophy.* New York: Washington Square Press, 1953.

Elliot, Anthony. *The Mourning of John Lennon.* Berkeley: University of California Press, 1999.

Epstein, Brian. *A Cellarful of Noise.* New York: Pocket Books, 1998.

Farrow, Mia. *What Falls Away.* New York: Doubleday, Nan A. Talese, 1997.

Fawcett, Anthony. *John Lennon: One Day at a Time.* New York: Grove, 1981.

Frankl, Viktor E. *Man's Search for Meaning.* New York: Washington Square, 1985.

Freud, Sigmund. *Civilization and Its Discontents.* Translated by James Strachey. New York: W. W. Norton, 1989.

Fromm, Erich. *Escape from Freedom.* New York: Henry Holt, 1994.

Garbarini, Vic, and Brian Cullman, with Barbara Graustark. *Strawberry Fields Forever: John Lennon Remembered.* New York: Bantam, Delilah, 1980.

Giuliano, Geoffrey, and Brenda Giuliano. *The Lost Lennon Interviews.* Holbrook, MA: Adams Media Corporation, 1996.

Graustark, Barbara. "The Real John Lennon." *Newsweek*, September 29, 1980.

Gross, Leonard. "John Lennon: A Shorn Beatle Tries it on His Own." *Look*, December 13, 1966.

Harrison, George. *I Me Mine.* New York: Simon and Schuster, 1980.

Harry, Bill. *The John Lennon Encyclopedia.* London: Virgin Publishing, 2000.

Hegel, Georg Wilhelm Friedrich. *The Philosophy of History*. Translated by J. Sibree. New York: Dover Publications, 1956.

Hoffer, Eric. *The True Believer*. New York: Harper, Perennial Library, 1966.

Hopkins, Jerry. *Yoko Ono*. New York: Macmillan, 1986.

Hunt, Chris, ed. "1000 Days of Revolution: The Beatles' Final Years—Jan 1, 1968 to Sept 27, 1970." *Mojo Special Limited Edition*, February 2003.

Johnson, Patricia Altenbernd. *On Heidegger*. Belmont, CA: Wadsworth, 2000.

Kant, Immanuel. "What is Enlightenment?" *Foundations of the Metaphysics of Morals*. Translated by Lewis White Beck. Indianapolis: Liberal Arts Press, 1959.

Kaufman, Walter, ed. *Existentialism from Dostoevsky to Sartre*. New York: Meridian, 1989.

Kierkegaard, Soren. *Fear and Trembling*. Translated by Alastair Hannay. New York: Viking Penguin, 1985.

Lavine, T. Z. *From Socrates to Sartre: The Philosophic Quest*. New York: Bantam, 1984.

Leary, Timothy, Ph.D., Ralph Metzner, Ph.D., and Richard Alpert, Ph.D. *The Psychedelic Experience: A Manual Based on the Tibetan Book of the Dead*. New York: Citadel Press, 1990.

Lennon: In My Life. Compilation. CD-ROM. England: Dressed To Kill, 1998.

Lennon, Cynthia. *A Twist of Lennon*. New York: Avon, 1980.

Lennon, John. *In His Own Write*. New York: Simon and Schuster, 1964.

———. *Skywriting by Word of Mouth*. New York: Harper and Row, 1986.

———. *Spaniard in the Works, A*. New York: Simon and Schuster, 1965.

Maccoby, Hyam. *The Mythmaker: Paul and the Invention of Christianity*. New York: Barnes and Noble, 1998.

MacHovec, Frank J., trans. *The Tibetan Book of the Dead*. Mount Vernon, NY: Peter Pauper, 1972.

Mascaró, Juan, trans. *The Bhagavad Gita.* New York: Penguin, 1985.

Mason, Paul. *The Maharishi.* Rockport, MA: Element, 1994.

Masters, Robert, and Jean Houston. *Mind Games: The Guide to Inner Space.* Wheaton, IL: Quest, 1998.

Miles, Bob, interviewer. *Testimony: The Life and Times of John Lennon in His Own Words.* CD-ROM. Buckinghamshire, UK: Magnum Music Group, 1995.

Navia, Luis E. *Diogenes of Sinope: The Man in the Tub.* Westport, CT: Greenwood, 1998.

Norman, Philip. *Shout! The Beatles in Their Generation.* New York: Simon and Schuster, Fireside, 1996.

O'Donnell, Jim. *The Day John Met Paul.* New York: Penguin, 1996.

Ono, Yoko. *Grapefruit.* New York: Simon and Schuster, 2000.

Phillips, Christopher. *Socrates Café.* New York: W. W. Norton, 2001.

Potts, Michel W. "Arun Gandhi Shares the Mahatma's Message." *India–West* 27, no. 13 (February 2002), A34.

Robertson, John. *The Art & Music of John Lennon.* London: Omnibus Press, 1990.

Rorty, Richard. *Contingency, Irony, and Solidarity.* New York: Cambridge University Press, 1989.

Russell, Bertrand. *Why I Am Not a Christian.* New York: Touchstone, 1957.

Sartre, Jean-Paul. *Existentialism and Human Emotions.* Secaucus, NJ: Carol Publishing, 1985.

Sauceda, James. *The Literary Lennon.* Ann Arbor, MI: Pierian Press, 1983.

Schonfield, Hugh. *The Passover Plot.* Rockport, MA: Element, 1994.

Sheff, David. *All We Are Saying.* New York: St. Martin's, Griffin, 2000.

Shotton, Pete, and Nicholas Schaffner. *John Lennon in My Life.* Briarcliff Manor, NY: Stein and Day, 1983.

Singer, Peter. *Hegel.* Oxford: Oxford University Press, 1989.

Solt, Andrew, and Sam Egan. *Imagine John Lennon*. New York: MacMillan, Sarah Lazin Books, 1988.

Stein, Joel. "Just Say Om." *Time*, August 4, 2003.

Stone, I. F. *The Trial of Socrates*. New York: Anchor Books, 1989.

Strathern, Paul. *Heidegger in 90 Minutes*. Chicago: Ivan R. Dee, 2002.

Stubbs, David. "We All Shine On." *Uncut*, November 2002.

Stuhr, John J. *Pragmatism, Postmodernism, and the Future of Philosophy*. New York: Routledge, 2003.

Taylor, A. E. *Socrates: The Man and His Thought*. Blackstone Audiobooks, 1993.

———. *The Mind of Plato*. Blackstone Audiobooks, 1993.

Turner, Steve. *The Gospel According to the Beatles*. Louisville: Westminster John Knox Press, 2006.

Wallechinsky, David, and Irving Wallace. *The People's Almanac*. Garden City, NY: Doubleday, 1975.

Wenner, Jann S. *Lennon Remembers*. New York: Verso, 2000.

Wiener, Jon. *Come Together: John Lennon in His Time*. Urbana and Chicago: Illini Books, 1991.

———. *Gimme Some Truth*. Berkeley and Los Angeles: University of California Press, 1999.

Wilson, A. N. *Paul: The Mind of the Apostle*. New York: W. W. Norton, 1998.

Wootton, Richard. *John Lennon*. New York: Random House, 1985.

Yogananda, Paramahansa. *Autobiography of a Yogi*. Los Angeles: Self Realization Fellowship, 2000.

INDEX

Quest Books

encourages open-minded inquiry into
world religions, philosophy, science, and the arts
in order to understand the wisdom of the ages,
respect the unity of all life, and help people explore
individual spiritual self-transformation.

Its publications are generously supported by
The Kern Foundation,
a trust committed to Theosophical education.

Quest Books is the imprint of
the Theosophical Publishing House,
a division of the Theosophical Society in America.
For information about programs, literature,
on-line study, membership benefits, and international centers,
see www.theosophical.org
or call 800-669-1571 or (outside the U.S.) 630-668-1571.

Related Quest Titles

Beyond Religion, by David N. Elkins
Karma, by Virginia Hanson,
with Shirley Nicholson and Rosemary Stewart
Manual for the Peacemaker, by Jean Houston,
with Margaret Rubin
The Meditative Path, by John Cianciosi
Mind Games, by Robert Masters, with Jean Houston
The Power of Thought, by John Algeo,
with Shirley J. Nicholson
The Vision Keepers, by Doug Alderson
War and the Soul, by Edward Tick

To order books or a complete Quest catalog,
call 800-669-9425 or (outside the U.S.) 630-665-0130.

Gary Tillery was born in Phoenix in 1947. Beginning in 1968, he served in Vietnam with the United States Air Force. When his enlistment was over in 1970, he earned a Bachelor's degree in Latin American Studies from Arizona State University and a Master's degree from the American Graduate School of International Management.

After two decades as co-owner of an advertising agency in suburban Chicago, Tillery turned to his lifelong passion for literature and art. He published a collection of interrelated short stories set in Vietnam titled *Darkling Plain* and began a series of humorous novels featuring "soft-boiled" detective Jack Savage—the first two titled *Death, Be Not Loud* and *To an Aesthete Dying Young*. Tillery's fascination with John Lennon led him to write *The Cynical Idealist*, in which he constructs a coherent view of Lennon's philosophy—one that was idealistic yet pragmatic.

Tillery is also a professional sculptor, using the traditional mediums of metal and stone to express contemporary ideas. His most prominent work is the sculpture for the Vietnam Memorial in Chicago. He has displayed in galleries from Pennsylvania to New Mexico and appeared in shows as far away as Shanghai. His works are in the private collections of Patricia DuPont and General Tommy Franks, and the National Vietnam Veterans Art Museum in Chicago possesses two pieces in its permanent collection.

Gary Tillery sheds a welcome new light on John Lennon as an artist, visionary, and catalyst for positive change in the world. In this "spiritual biography," Tillery creates a new art form and reveals Lennon's essence and core values as no other biographer has. He celebrates Lennon without idealizing him and reminds us why his music and message still matter—and will continue to matter for generations to come.

—**Joe Raiola**, Producer,
Theatre Within's Annual John Lennon Tribute